D0978910

Praise for
SAVING YOUR MARRIAGE BEFORE IT STARTS

"Every engaged and newlywed couple needs to read this book by Les and Leslie. And while you're at it, don't miss out on the incredible SYMBIS Assessment. It's fantastic!"

Shaunti Feldhahn, Social researcher and
author of *For Women Only* and *For Men Only*

"This program is incredibly practical, easy to use, and long overdue."

H. Norman Wright, Author of *Before You Say "I Do"*

"Les and Leslie are the go-to couple for launching lifelong love. *Saving Your Marriage Before It Starts* is right on the money."

Dave Ramsey, Founder of Financial Peace University

"You simply can't afford to miss out on all that SYMBIS has to offer. I've personally benefited from it."

Gary Smalley, Author of *The Language of Love*

"We love Les and Leslie. They are our go-to couple for all things marriage prep. You will love the SYMBIS book and workbooks. And their SYMBIS Assessment is a must-do."

Judah Smith, Author of *Life Is* _____.

"I wish every engaged and newly married couple would use *Saving Your Marriage Before It Starts*. It's fresh, relevant, and extremely practical."

Dr. Neil Clark Warren, Founder of eHarmony

RESOURCES BY LES AND LESLIE PARROTT

3 Seconds (by Les)

The Complete Guide to Marriage Mentoring (and workbooks and video)

The Control Freak (by Les)

Crazy Good Sex (by Les)

Dot.com Dating

The First Drop of Rain (by Leslie)

Getting Ready for the Wedding

God Loves You Nose to Toes (children's book by Leslie)

The Good Fight

Helping Your Struggling Teenager (by Les)

High Maintenance Relationships (by Les)

The Hour That Matters Most

I Love You More (and workbooks and video)

L.O.V.E.

The Love List

Love Talk (and workbooks and video)

Love Talk Devotional

Making Happy

Meditations on Proverbs for Couples

The Parent You Want to Be

Questions Couples Ask

Real Relationships (and workbook and video)

Saving Your Marriage Before It Starts (and workbooks and video)

Saving Your Second Marriage Before It Starts (and workbooks and video)

Seven Secrets of a Healthy Dating Relationship (by Les)

Soul Friends (by Leslie)

Trading Places (and workbooks)

You Matter More Than You Think (by Leslie)

You're Stronger Than You Think (by Les)

Your Time-Starved Marriage (and workbooks and video)

SAVING YOUR
SECOND
MARRIAGE
BEFORE IT STARTS

SAVING YOUR SECOND MARRIAGE BEFORE IT STARTS

*Nine Questions to Ask Before —
and After — You Remarry*

NEWLY EXPANDED EDITION

Drs. Les & Leslie Parrott

#1 *New York Times* Bestselling Authors

ZONDERVAN®

ZONDERVAN

Saving Your Second Marriage Marriage Before It Starts
Copyright © 2001, 2015 by Les and Leslie Parrott

This title is also available as a Zondervan ebook. Visit www.zondervan.com/ebooks.

Requests for information should be addressed to:
Zondervan, 3900 *Sparks Dr. SE, Grand Rapids, Michigan 49546*

Library of Congress Cataloging-in-Publication Data

Parrott, Les.
    Saving your second marriage before it starts : nine questions to ask before (and after)
you remarry / Les and Leslie Parrott
      p. cm.
    ISBN 978-0-310-34630-2
     1. Remarriage. 2. Stepfamilies. 3. Marriage counseling. I. Parrott, Leslie L., 1964 –
II. Title.
    HQ1018 .P37   2001
    306.84—dc21   2001026749

All Scripture quotations, unless otherwise indicated, are taken from The Holy Bible, *New International Version®, NIV®.* Copyright © 1973, 1978, 1984, 2011 by Biblica, Inc.® Used by permission. All rights reserved worldwide.

Scripture quotations marked CEV are taken from the *Contemporary English Version.* Copyright © 1995 by American Bible Society. Used by permission.

Scripture quotations marked MSG are taken from *The Message.* Copyright © 1993, 1994, 1995, 1996, 2000, 2001, 2002. Used by permission of NavPress Publishing Group.

Any Internet addresses (websites, blogs, etc.) and telephone numbers in this book are offered as a resource. They are not intended in any way to be or imply an endorsement by Zondervan, nor does Zondervan vouch for the content of these sites and numbers for the life of this book.

All rights reserved. No part of this publication may be reproduced, stored in a retrieval system, or transmitted in any form or by any means — electronic, mechanical, photocopy, recording, or any other — except for brief quotations in printed reviews, without the prior permission of the publisher.

Published in association with Yates & Yates, www.yates2.com.

Cover design: Ranjy Thomas / Flying Rhino
Cover photography: © Surkov Vladimir / Shutterstock®
Interior design: Kait Lamphere & Ryan Farmer

First printing August 2015 / Printed in the United States of America

To our SYMBIS Facilitators

Whether you are a pastor, counselor, chaplain, or marriage mentor, you shaped not only this book but the SYMBIS Assessment. Your investment in helping couples launch lifelong love as a SYMBIS Facilitator will impact generations to come.

Hang my locket around your neck,
wear my ring on your finger.
Love is invincible facing danger and death.
Passion laughs at the terrors of hell.
The fire of love stops at nothing —
it sweeps everything before it.
Flood waters can't drown love,
torrents of rain can't put it out.

SONG OF SONGS 8:6 – 7

CONTENTS

WORKBOOK EXERCISES

BELOW IS A LISTING of the exercises and self-tests you will find in the two workbooks we have designed to go along with this book (one for men and one for women). In each chapter we will point you to a specific exercise to enjoy once you have read a particular section. This list can serve as a quick reference to the location of the exercises within the book.

BEFORE YOU BEGIN

"HOW CAN I AVOID the same problems that plagued my first marriage?" Sarah asked this question during a break at one of our marriage seminars. "Tom and I are getting married in a few months—we're very much in love—but we both know it's not going to be a cakewalk."

Sarah went on to tell us that her first marriage ended after just three years when her husband walked out on her for reasons that are still a mystery. "Maybe we were too young, I don't know," she confessed, "but I do know that this time I have my eyes open, and we want to do everything we can to ensure lifelong love together." She asked again, "What do I need to know as a person who's getting married for the second time?"

The seminar was about to begin so we had to postpone our answer for Sarah. We eventually spoke with her and Tom at length over the lunch break. We learned that Tom was coming from a nine-year marriage that ended when his wife died of cancer. We also learned that he was bringing two young children into his new marriage with Sarah. "Do you have any tips for helping the kids make a smooth adjustment to all this?" Tom asked us. "And what should we do about his parents?" Sarah chimed in. "They think we're rushing into this marriage."

Needless to say, we didn't have time to do justice to the many questions Sarah and Tom had about starting their second marriage. And truth be told, we didn't feel all that confident about what little advice we did have. We passed along a few bits of information and underscored the importance of healing the wounds from their previous marriages. But both Les and I felt bad that we could not do more to help Sarah and Tom get started on the right foot—for the second time.

That was more than a half dozen years ago. Since that time, we have dedicated much of our professional lives to helping couples like Sarah and Tom build the best marriages possible. Up until that time we had worked with countless couples entering marriage for the first time, but it wasn't until we met Sarah and Tom that we began to realize that we were neglecting critically important concerns for nearly half of all couples marrying today. We realized that these couples, where one or both were marrying for a second time, faced a unique set of circumstances that desperately needed attention. These couples needed a special set of skills for saving their second marriage before and after it started.

Well, since you're reading this book, we know that you have a story that is in some way similar to Sarah's and Tom's. You may or may not be bringing kids into your new marriage. You may or may not have been wounded in a previous relationship. We don't know the details of your story. But we know for sure that you want your marriage to afford you every good thing it was designed to give. And it can—in spite of the odds.

FOR BETTER OR WORSE?

Let's be honest. The "till death do us part" of the marriage vow rings increasingly ironic. In the 1930s, one out of seven marriages ended in divorce. In the 1960s, it was one out of four. Of the 2.4 million couples who will get married this year in the United States, it is predicted that at least 50 percent of the marriages will not survive. And most startling, of those getting married for a second time, 60 percent will not make it. For too many couples, marriage has become "till divorce do us part."

Every couple marrying today is at risk. More than two hundred thousand new marriages each year end prior to the couple's second anniversary, and that number is even higher for remarried couples. After they toss the bouquets and return the tuxedos, couples often assume they're headed for marital bliss. But a study of those who recently tied the knot revealed that 49 percent reported having serious marital problems. Half were already having doubts about whether their marriages would last.[1]

How can this be? The professional community has never known more than we know today about how to build a successful marriage. Yet marriages continue to crumble. Perhaps the main reason is that couples—unlike you and your partner—are simply not taking advantage of the terrific tools available to those who seek them. In fact, less than a fifth of all marriages in America are preceded by some kind of formal marriage preparation.[2] And couples marrying again too often feel they have learned from their mistakes and naively believe they are older and wiser the second time around.

We have a hunch you're looking for a different approach. And this book offers one.

HOW TO PREDICT A HAPPY REMARRIAGE

Over the last two decades, marriage specialists have researched the ingredients of a happy marriage. As a result, we know more about building a successful marriage today than ever before. For example, happily married couples will have:

- healthy expectations of marriage
- a realistic concept of love
- a positive attitude and outlook toward life
- the ability to communicate their feelings
- an understanding and acceptance of their gender differences
- the ability to make decisions and settle arguments

- a common spiritual foundation and goal
- a deep and abiding commitment and covenant together

And for those marrying the second time around with kids from their first marriage, there are a couple additional characteristics:

- knowledge of what it takes to combine a family
- stepparenting skills

In short, the things that forecast a healthy remarriage form the basis of the nine questions we pose in this book. Every couple should be aware of these issues before (and after) they marry. Taking the time to understand these issues is like investing in an insurance policy against divorce—especially if you're entering marriage for the second time around.

A PERSONAL NOTE ON REMARRIAGE

Shortly after *Saving Your Marriage Before It Starts* (SYMBIS) was first published, we began getting requests for information from couples who had become engaged after one or both of them was in a previous marriage that ended either in death or divorce. These couples, on the brink of entering a second marriage, knew there were issues and struggles ahead of them that were unique to their situation—compared to couples getting married for the first time. After all, some of them had children they would be bringing with them into their new marriage. Others had baggage from a previous marriage; either they were enveloped by grief from the loss of a spouse or they felt burned by a spouse who had hurt them deeply. And still others were entering a second marriage with more than a little anxiety and wanted to be sure they did everything they could to ensure success the second time around.

At the urging of these couples, we began considering the needs of remarried couples. What we found compelled us to revise and expand *Saving Your Marriage Before It Starts* to address the needs of those marrying again. The result is the book you now hold in your hands. Seventy-five percent of those who divorce will marry again. Remarriage is nearly as common as first marriages, yet more than 60 percent of remarriages end in divorce. What's more, second marriages in which there are children in the family are twice as likely to end in divorce as remarriages in which there are no children.[3]

But it was another single piece of information that really made our hearts sink: *Many remarried couples conclude within the first months that their new marriage is failing, when, in fact, studies have shown that the estimated time it takes to adapt to being a stepfamily ranges from two to seven years.*

Allow us to say it bluntly: Remarried couples face a rocky road. Experience, unfortunately, is not the best predictor of success when it comes to marriage. That's not to say that you are bound to have major difficulties. Not by a long shot. In fact, we believe that by going through this book and the accompanying men's and women's workbooks—by taking the time for proper preparation—you can make your second marriage a first-class success.

SAY GOOD-BYE TO GUESSWORK

Saving Your Second Marriage Before It Starts is based on the fact that marriage doesn't have to be a gamble. As a psychologist (Les) and a marriage and family therapist (Leslie) who have counseled hundreds of married and remarried couples, we have learned that living happily ever after is less a mystery than the mastery of certain skills. Although married life will always have its difficulties, you will steadily and dramatically improve your relationship by mastering certain life skills.

Many couples wrongly blame in-laws, money, and sex for breakups and marital dissatisfaction. However, the hot points in marriage usually result from poor communication, gender issues, and lack of spiritual health, to name a few. This book cuts to the heart of every marital conflict. Whether you are single and dating, in a committed relationship, contemplating marriage, or already ensconced in one, this book will help you learn the skills you'll need for a lasting and happy life together—*before* unhappiness sets in.

We have written two workbooks as companions to this book, one for the man and one for the woman. The twenty-six self-tests in the workbooks will help you and your partner put into action what is taught in this book. As an additional help, we have provided questions for reflection at the end of each chapter that are suitable as discussion starters for couples or small groups.

If you would like to bring this program to your church or small group setting, or even use it to augment your personal experience, a DVD kit, also entitled *Saving Your Second Marriage Before It Starts, Newly Expanded Edition*, is available.

We wrote this book from our hearts. We feel passionately about giving a new generation of remarried couples the chance to go back to square one and learn the rudiments of lifelong marriage. In the process, you will discover the deepest and most radical expression of intimacy two people can know.

TAKING THE SYMBIS ASSESSMENT

One of the best ways to make the content of this book deeply relevant to your relationship is to take the SYMBIS Assessment. It takes just thirty minutes to complete online (each of you answers questions separately) and provides a powerful and personalized fifteen-page report. You'll discover your unique strengths as a couple and how your two personalities mesh (see Appendix). In short, the SYMBIS Assessment gives you every possible advantage for launching lifelong love, and it's sure to bring your relationship to a deeper level of intimacy.

In fact, if you purchased this book you can use the unique code (specific to this book) to obtain a discount. *Your unique code is located on the inside of the book's dust jacket.* The code is only good for one use by a couple.

Because the SYMBIS Assessment is so robust, you'll need a certified SYMBIS Facilitator to guide you through your results.[*]

Using the assessment is not required. It's simply an option that we think you will appreciate. Simply go to **SYMBISassessment.com** to learn more.

By the way, we will note specific places within each chapter where the SYMBIS Assessment will have particular relevance to your relationship. Here's the first one:

SYMBIS Report Page 2
What's Your Marriage Momentum?

Every engaged and newlywed couple has momentum. It's a quick read on all you have going for you in marriage. And when you know how much momentum you have, it makes the road of romance as smooth and pleasurable as possible. If you're using the SYMBIS Assessment with your book, you'll discover your marriage momentum in your personalized report.

You can find the assessment at SYMBISassessment.com.

OUR PRAYER FOR YOU

Few experiences in life are more meaningful, precious, and personal as pledging your hearts to each other in marriage. And if you are a person of faith, if you strive to walk in the footsteps of Jesus, we know you ultimately long for a God-honoring covenant of marriage. You want to infuse your dreams of love with God's way of living.

"What happens when we live God's way?" Paul writes in Galatians. "He brings gifts into our lives, much the same way

---

[*] If you are already working with a counselor or pastor and they are not certified, we can help them become certified to use the assessment with you. They can do so at SYMBISassessment.com.

that fruit appears in an orchard—things like affection for others, exuberance about life, serenity. We develop a willingness to stick with things, a sense of compassion in the heart, and a conviction that a basic holiness permeates things and people. We find ourselves involved in loyal commitments, not needing to force our way in life, able to marshal and direct our energies wisely."[4]

Who wouldn't want all of these rich gifts to infuse their married life? That's why we dedicate the final chapter of *Saving Your Second Marriage Before It Starts* to helping you do just that. But you don't have to wait for the last chapter. We have written a Bible study to accompany this book (as well as the SYMBIS Assessment) that you can access right now:

- For the nine-day Bible study (one study for each chapter) accompanying this book, go to:
  http://SYMB.IS/RemarriedPlan
- For the fifteen-day Bible study (one study for each page of your SYMBIS Report) accompanying the SYMBIS Assessment, go to:
  http://SYMB.IS/AssessmentPlan

Our prayer for you, wherever you are on your faith journey, is that you would enjoy all the fruit and every blessing your marriage has to offer. We wrote this book from our hearts. We feel passionately about giving a new generation of couples the chance to go back to "square one" and learn the rudiments of lifelong marriage. In the process, you will discover the deepest and most radical expression of intimacy two people can know.

LES AND LESLIE PARROTT
SEATTLE, WASHINGTON

Question One

ARE YOU READY TO GET MARRIED AGAIN?

He who chooses the beginning of a road chooses the place it leads to.
HARRY EMERSON FOSDICK

"This is going to be a challenge," Debbie said as we wrangled a dozen toddlers together for a foot race. It was little Nick's third birthday, and all his buddies wanted to see who could run the fastest.

Once they were lined up in a semiorderly fashion, I shouted the universal words to get them going: "On your mark, get set, go!" They took off like rockets. Well, sort of. I mean, they began moving forward. Most of them, anyway. But some of the little ones just stood there, oblivious to the race they were in until they saw the other kids running.

Ever felt like one of those kids? Have you ever wanted to race, but when the starting gun sounds, you realize you're not really ready? This first chapter is a kind of insurance policy against this experience for anyone entering a second marriage. Of course, if you are already in a second marriage, you will still find this chapter useful because we will explore some of the specific challenges you're already facing or will shortly. Either way, whether you are simply considering a second marriage or already ensconced in one, we dedicate this chapter to helping you measure your preparedness for it. And we begin with a mini self-test.

Take a moment right now to answer these half-dozen true/false questions as honestly as you can.

True or False   I want to get married again because I'll feel less lonely.

True or False   It's not fair to my kids to not have a mom *and* a dad in the house.

True or False   Remarriage will help me heal the pain from my past.

True or False   I would be better off financially if I were married again.

True or False   I feel pressure from friends and/or family to get married again.

True or False   I want to remarry because I want to have a child (or more children).

If you answered "true" to any of these questions, there is good reason for you to read this chapter and see just what it can do to better equip you for a second marriage. Why? Because each of these statements represents one of the fundamental fallacies about remarriage. We know, for example, that the person who enters a marriage to improve his financial position or to have babies is getting remarried for the wrong reasons. Same is true for the person who remarries to feel less lonely or to erase the pain from the past. Now, let's be honest, remarriage may very well do some of these things. It may make you feel less lonely or it may increase your bank balance. But that's not the issue. The issue is motivation.

A FEW REASONS PEOPLE SHOULDN'T GET MARRIED AGAIN

Ask most people why they are getting married—for the first or the second time—and the answer is nearly reflexive: "Because we are in love." But if you scratch the surface, you'll find that the motivations for matrimony are far more complex. A combination of many complicated situations and needs motivates most people to marry, with some motivations being better than others. In fact, some reasons for marrying improve your chances of success while others work against it—especially when it comes to marrying for the second time.

So before we go much further in helping you assess your personal readiness for remarriage, we'll take a brief look at a few terrible reasons why people remarry. We'll then take a closer look at the primary positive reason for marriage that increases the probability of relational longevity and success the second time around.

LOVE AT FIRST SIGHT

Love at first sight seems like a romantic reason for marriage, but it's not a good predictor of marital success. This is especially true for a second marriage that is supposed to be "magically" different from the first. Not that strong feelings of attraction cannot occur early in a relationship; they do. But such feelings alone provide a weak foundation for a long-lasting relationship. Just ask the dozens of Hollywood remarriages each year that are ignited on a studio lot and break up after only a year or two of wedded disaster.

ON THE REBOUND

Being on the rebound also does not bode well for marital success. It's a proven fact that people tend to fall in love more easily when they have recently been rejected by someone they once loved. Researchers have known for years that people suffer low self-esteem after a divorce and are far less discriminating in choosing a partner as they are trying to cope with their loss.[1] To marry on the rebound is undesirable because the wedding occurs as a reaction to a previous partner, rather than being based on real love for the new one.

REBELLION

Rebellion leads some into a remarriage mismatch. Getting even with an ex-spouse, for example, by marrying someone the ex knowingly does not like, is not uncommon, but it's always costly. The interference of a former spouse can actually increase feelings of romantic attraction between partners, because it gives the new couple a common enemy. As with marriage on the rebound, however, the wedding is a response to someone else rather than to one's partner.

LONELINESS

Loneliness can sometimes drive a person into a hasty marriage. This is especially true among the divorced and widowed.[2] The problem with this motivation is that lonely people will end up lonely in marriage if the relationship doesn't have much more to stand on. In other words, it is the relationship rather than the institution of marriage that banishes loneliness.

OBLIGATION

Obligation sometimes substitutes for love when people consider remarriage. Some partners marry because one of them feels guilty about breaking it off. Others marry because they think their children need a father or a mother. Some people even marry as a kind of crusade, like the woman who marries a widower to help him overcome his grief. Such marriages don't often work. The pitied partner comes to resent being the object of a crusade.

FINANCIAL ADVANCEMENT

Financial advancement is a remarriage motivator for some, especially young divorced mothers who consider remarriage primarily because they are exhausted from the struggle of supporting and caring for their small children.[3] Men, too, can marry to advance their career in some professions. The person going into marriage mainly for economic reasons, however, is not a likely candidate for marrying well.

> Immature love says, "I love you because I need you." Mature love says, "I need you because I love you."
>
> Erich Fromm

SEXUAL ATTRACTION

Sexual attraction and guilt over sexual involvement are popular but weak reasons for marriage. Sex is not a sufficient reason to marry and seldom leads to lifelong happiness. In fact, the sexual chemistry between two people often blinds the partners to other important relational qualities. We'll have more to say about this later in the chapter.

ESCAPE

Escape is perhaps the most damaging motivation for remarriage. Sociologists have a name for it these days: serial monogamy. Some people marry with the hope that a new person or a new situation will be better. This is a terrible basis for marriage. It can start a long series of relational failures. These people believe that a new relationship could not be worse than their present one, or that their situation couldn't possibly be worse than what it is—and they are almost always surprised to find out that, with their remarriage, it is.

PRESSURE

Pressure from parents, peers, and society in general pushes some divorced or widowed people into marriage. Research shows that this can be particularly true for women. The more one is identified as a couple, the more difficult it is to back out of an engagement. As you may well know, however, breaking an engagement is less stressful than divorcing later or being unhappily married.

> Those who marry to escape something usually find something else.
>
> Claire Hutchet Bishop

Well, there you have it, a few reasons *not* to get married again. After reading this list, you may be feeling like there's nearly no good reason to get married. Not true. We have a good friend, Dr. Neil Clark Warren, who is fond of saying people need to fall in love for all the right reasons. And we couldn't agree more. There are some right reasons to remarry, and there is one in particular that really matters. But before we reveal it, we want to encourage you to complete Exercise 1 in the accompanying workbooks (there's one for men and one for women) designed to go along with *Saving Your Second Marriage Before It Starts*. Like most of the exercises in these workbooks, it will take you only a few minutes.

Workbook Exercise 1
The Remarriage Motivation Test

Why we do what we do is one of the most important elements in human relationships. And one of the most neglected too. The workbook exercise *The Remarriage Motivation Test* will help you pinpoint the reasons — good or bad — that may be leading you into a second marriage. And with this understanding you will be miles down the road in being able to apply much of the content you'll discover in this book.

THE MOST IMPORTANT
REMARRIAGE MOTIVATOR

We have seen that rebounding, rebellion, escape, loneliness, obligation, sex, pressure, and all the rest are not likely predictors of a happy second marriage. In fact, any one of them should give you pause if you are primarily motivated by one. Postponing a marriage date, for example, may give you the time you need to consider why you are getting married again in the first place. By the way, it's not a shame to break off an engagement to reconsider your motivations. About one in four engaged couples break up temporarily for that very reason.[4] We did.

After six and a half years of dating and nearly five months of being engaged, I (Leslie) was having second thoughts. Can you believe it? Once Les proposed to me, I said yes without thinking about it. Literally. We had dated so long that I was taking our relationship, as well as our eventual marriage, for granted. We never shopped together for wedding rings, and the night in Chicago that Les surprised me with his proposal was terribly romantic. I said yes out of instinct. After it was official and we were engaged, however, I began feeling as though I hadn't really decided on marriage for myself. It felt more like it was Les's decision and his timing, not ours, that was taking us to the chapel. My doubts were strong enough for me to break it off, at least temporarily, and see a counselor. A month or two later the decision to get married was as much mine as it was his. That was 1984, and since then neither of us has ever doubted the decision to marry each other.

Part of the reason for our marital success may be that we married, not out of a deficit, but out of a motivation that researchers say is the most important: *companionship*.[5] To love and be loved by another person is perhaps the single most satisfying experience on earth. Many of the benefits of companionship can be enjoyed without marriage, of course, but marriage provides the social structure for experiencing this phenomenon most deeply. It provides a configuration, a form, an institution for two souls to walk together through life. It provides a covenant whereby soul mates pledge to love each other in good times and in bad, in sickness and in health—to have and to hold as companions unto death.

Our prayer is that you and your partner are getting remarried for all the right reasons, that your marital motivations are pure. And if that's the case, it's now time to turn your attention to your remarriage readiness.

MARKS OF REMARRIAGE READINESS

A second wedding—sometimes known as "the encore wedding"—no longer necessarily means a quick and quiet trip to city hall. "This time I made a promise to really have *fun* at my own wedding," Deborah said. "At first we worried about overdoing things or underplaying something else. Then we just went for it. We wanted to host a celebration, and we did."

Deborah is not alone among second-time brides. While it's not true for every couple getting married again, many are spending plenty of time, energy, and money on preparing for a second wedding that was everything they wanted for their first and didn't get. This kind of preparation may not be bad, but don't let it delude you into thinking it makes you ready to get remarried. You may have a beautiful diamond ring. You may be holding two airline tickets to a romantic honeymoon getaway. You may have sent out calligraphy invitations to a hundred of your closest family and friends. You may have your wedding planned down to the finest little detail, but the truth remains: *Being prepared for your wedding does not equal being prepared for your marriage.*

It's understandable that some couples spend more time preparing for their weddings than they do for their marriage. Wedding plans seem far more tangible. Once the caterer is scheduled, you can check it off your to-do list. Relational readiness is not so tidy. In recent years, however, experts have made great strides in identifying the qualities that reveal whether or not a couple is really ready for marriage—for the first or second time. And if you didn't get these right the first time, you have a terrific chance to get them right before you remarry. You can think of these findings as a kind of checklist—a checklist divided into two parts: personal readiness and relational readiness.

> People are always asking couples whose marriage has endured at least a quarter of a century for their secret for success. Actually, it is no secret at all. I am a forgiving woman. Long ago, I forgave my husband for not being Paul Newman.
>
> Erma Bombeck

PERSONAL READINESS FOR REMARRIAGE

Walk into the office of any marriage expert and ask what personal qualities are most important for the soon-to-be spouse in a second marriage and you may get an earful. The list, to say the least, would be long. But if we were to boil all of the responses down to a minimum, you would probably end up with at least these two: a healthy self-concept and independence from your first marriage.

Self-concept refers to your mental and emotional well-being, and it's built on two qualities: knowing who you are and liking who you are. A mountain of research shows that a fragile self-concept leaves one susceptible to a marital mismatch (as well as personal problems such as depression), while a healthy self-concept (for both you and your partner) is predictive of a fully functioning marriage — one that will not only go the distance but also be extremely fulfilling. When conflict arises, for example, two people with a healthy self-concept have the internal resources required to work it out. Those with a poor self-concept are prone to deny the conflict exists or react defensively to any suggestion of compromise. They don't have the emotional reserves to navigate the inevitable tough times, and the marriage pays the price.

We mentioned earlier our friend Dr. Neil Clark Warren. He has written extensively about this fact in his wonderful book *Finding the Love of Your Life*. One night over dinner, we asked Neil why he gives so much attention to a person's self-concept before they get married. He didn't hesitate for a minute. "A marriage can only be as healthy as the least healthy person in that partnership," he answered. How true. In a very real sense, a lack of emotional well-being is hazardous to your marriage. So we echo the sentiments of our friend Neil: Get healthy before you get remarried.

Independence is all about your relationship with your former spouse. Your relationship with him or her has shaped your ability to relate to your second spouse more than you might think. At conscious and unconscious levels, your first spouse taught you to either trust or not, to be intimate or stay distant, to express your feelings or keep them private.

Much of your personal readiness for remarriage depends on the state of your relationship with your former spouse, whether they are deceased or you are divorced. What lessons from your first marriage will you bring into your second marriage? Is there unresolved pain in relation to your first spouse that you still need to work through? The point is that before reentering marriage, you need to carefully examine the baggage you are bringing with you. We'll explore more of this later in this chapter as we talk about the unique challenges you might face if you are divorced versus widowed and entering a second marriage.

RELATIONAL READINESS FOR REMARRIAGE

Assessing the personal qualities of self-concept and independence is only half of the journey toward determining your marital readiness. The second half has to do, not with personal qualities, but with the relational qualities you share with your partner. Once again we whittle away at a long list to examine the bare essentials. If you and your partner are ready for remarriage, your relationship will be characterized by longevity, stability, and similarity.

Longevity has to do with how long you have known each other and dated. We work on a university campus and have discovered a disturbing syndrome afflicting a good portion of every senior class. We call it the "ring-by-spring" syndrome. That's the humorous way of putting it. But when two people decide to jump into marriage too quickly—whether college students or mature adults—it's no laughing matter.

Research on mate selection makes it clear: Couples who rush into matrimony are at significant risk. A study conducted at Kansas State University reveals that a strong correlation exists between length of time spent dating and marital satisfaction. The researchers discovered that "couples who had dated for more than two years scored consistently high on marital satisfaction, while couples who had dated for shorter periods scored in a wide range from very high to very low."[6] The longer you date, the more ready you are for remarriage.

If you have been dating for less than two years, it doesn't mean you are predestined to dissatisfaction in marriage. It just means the risk of that happening is higher. So why take the risk? We understand that the time you have been together may be the most romantic months you could ever dream of, and we understand that being remarried might seem to alleviate some financial stress, or be "good for the kids," but there is no need to rush. Give yourselves time, and you will increase your chances of sharing a married love that will go the distance.

Stability is defined as the quality of having constancy, reliability, dependability, and steadfastness. If these terms characterize your relationship, that's a good sign. Far too many unsteady couples wobble and warble their way to the altar—as if just getting there was the point. It's not. The point is to get there in a stable and steadfast condition. Why? Once again, this quality increases the probability of fulfillment in a second marriage. Couples whose courtships are characterized by conflict, turbulence, and those telltale on-again-off-again starts and stops—in a word, instability—are far less likely to find happiness in marriage.

Stability in the dating years indicates that a couple is learning to practice negotiation and compromise. They are learning the fine art and skill of communication. In short, stable couples are proving to themselves in the dating years that they can navigate the turbulent and treacherous waters that are an inevitable part of sailing a second marriage vessel. These couples are resolving conflicts and keeping an even keel. They are charting a steady course that is bound to bring them happiness.

Similarity is not about feeling and doing everything in exactly the same way. That's uniformity. Similarity is more like unity than uniformity. It has to do with holding common values, beliefs, and attitudes. Why is similarity important to your marriage? Because the happiest married couples have a lot in common. You may disagree, but it's a fact. Similarities—especially on the issues that matter most to each person—are the superglue that holds them together. The more similarities two people share, the more likely their relationship will survive and thrive. It's that simple. After a careful review of many, many marital studies, researchers concluded that "similarity is associated with marital success and is less associated with marital instability and divorce."[7]

If a happy and committed couple has a lot in common, you may be wondering just what exactly these commonalties are. Role expectations for husband and wife certainly make the list. So do common values about spiritual matters, money, family, and even politics. Other similarities to consider are desire for children, energy level, dependability, sense of humor, cleanliness, goals, interests, habits, and skills.[8] The list is practically endless.

Well, does this emphasis on unity mean you shouldn't marry someone who is very different from you? Not necessarily. But having plenty of important similarities can outweigh and counteract your dissimilarities. Economic, racial, religious, political, intellectual, educational, and emotional similarities provide a common base of operation and make life significantly easier to negotiate together. Why? Because every difference requires time, energy, and work to find a middle ground, if there is one. The more differences between you, the more nooks and crannies you will discover in your relationship for resentment and frustration to take hold. And the more stressful your second marriage becomes.

> It is very important to make sure the person you're marrying is like-minded. It's crucial for a couple to have shared goals and values. The more you have in common, the less you have to argue about.
>
> Barbara Friedman

So as you consider your relational readiness for remarriage, take time to examine your longevity, your stability, and your differences. The time you spend on this today may save you a lot of pain in the future. And you'll find more fulfillment in the present as you discover both your personal and relational readiness for lifelong love in a second marriage.

Before we close this first chapter, we want to address your specific situation as you ask yourself whether you are ready for remarriage. What follows is some tailored advice for the spouse who has been divorced and the spouse who has been widowed. We also offer some guidance for the person who has not been married before but is marrying someone in one of these two categories. Feel free to go right to the section that applies to you.

FOR THE PERSON WHO'S BEEN DIVORCED

There is a myth about divorce that it is a temporary crisis whose most harmful impact is at the time of the breakup. Truth is, the pain of divorce lingers a lifetime. Its sting is reexperienced again and again. And not even falling in love and marrying for the second time erases that. This is not to say that a second marriage may not help ease the pain, but know this: Remarriage does not make the lingering pain of divorce disappear completely.

Maybe you did know that. But what you might not know is that because you are divorced you are most likely entering a second marriage with a bag full of guilt, whether true or false, real or imaginary. Every divorced person we know feels guilty for the failure of their first marriage—whether they filed or the other person filed for it. For both parties, guilt is simply endemic to divorce. And this guilt can't help but to enter your second marriage.

For this reason we encourage you to explore this guilt with your new partner and with a trusted counselor if necessary. Why? Because guilt has a way of seeping down into the crevices of our relationships and doing damage we can't even see. Guilt, if allowed to run wild, dismantles love. It prevents us from being authentic and genuine.

Renee is a good example. She entered her second marriage oblivious to the guilt she carried with her. Three years later, she stood on the brink of a second divorce because she had suddenly changed. Her husband was mystified. "You're not yourself anymore," he'd say. And he was right. Renee had spent the past three years of her marriage trying to accommodate him in any way she could. The guilt she brought into this second marriage was the fuel in her tank, and it drove her to do everything for him she hadn't done for her first husband. But she could only keep it up so long. By year three she had burned out.

> **Workbook Exercise 2**
> **The Remarriage Readiness Questionnaire**
>
> Now that you have studied some of the most important predictors of remarriage success, you will find it valuable to apply them to your own situation. The workbook exercise *The Remarriage Readiness Questionnaire* will help you measure your personal readiness for remarriage. But the quiz you will find here will only be as valuable as you are honest while taking it, especially as you compare your score with your partner's.

Guilt can do that to a person. It can drive you into behaviors as a way of paying penitence when all that is required is the real you. So if you are entering this second marriage as a divorced person, take a good look at your backpack of guilt. Make sure you know what it might be causing you to do. Maybe you are bringing into your second marriage financial debt that is shrouded in guilt. This debt could cause you to be a workaholic. Maybe it's guilt over not being the kind of parent you want to be. Or guilt over a lack of physical passion on your part. Whatever it is, identify it and explore it. With a little exploration, you can reduce guilt's impact before it dismantles your relationship.

FOR THE PERSON WHO'S BEEN WIDOWED

Linda and Jeff, both in their forties, were coming to us for premarital counseling. But on this particular day, Linda said she wanted to see us alone. She brought her diary into our counseling office and said, "I want to read you what I wrote this morning." She cleared her throat and put on her reading glasses. "Wednesday, 8:30 A.M.; I awoke to the phone ringing. I didn't answer. Instead I'm jolted back into the experience of answering that very same phone four years ago when my thirteen-year-old daughter, Cindy, called to say that Ted had collapsed while watching her soccer practice that morning at school. He'd been taken to the hospital. I raced to be by his side, but it was too late. Cindy met me in the parking lot, sobbing. I was numb. Some days, like today, I still am. How could Ted be gone? If he were here we'd be celebrating our twenty-fifth wedding anniversary tonight."

At that point, Linda closed her diary, wiped the tears brimming in her eyes, and asked, "Should I really be getting married again?" We sat still for a moment. She continued, "I mean, I love Jeff, I really do, but would Ted want me to do this?"

It's a familiar question to anyone who has worked with a widow or widower about to be married. Just like the person who's been divorced, the person whose spouse has died carries plenty of guilt into a second marriage. "Is this fair to his memory?" "Would she approve of this person?" "And what about our sex life? Part of me just doesn't feel right." These are all comments and questions we've heard many times. And chances are you are asking them too. We aren't going to answer them for you. Only you can do that. But we can tell you that we've known many people who got a second start at marriage after their first spouse died. They created a beautiful second marriage that made the rest of their life fulfilling.

So if you are in this category and you are wrestling with guilt and grief and other troubling emotions because you lost your first spouse to circumstances beyond your control, we encourage you to process them with an objective counselor. Typically, a couple sessions is enough to articulate your feelings and get some clarity for your future. And with clarity you will be able to shed some unnecessary baggage, preserve the memory and honor of the spouse you lost, and begin to create a new future.

FOR THE PERSON WHO'S MARRYING SOMEONE WHO HAS BEEN MARRIED BEFORE

If you fall into this category, we want to commend you for taking the time to read this book with your partner. It says a great deal about your character and your desire for a solid marriage. And since you are entering marriage for the first time with someone who, in a sense, already knows the ropes, you will have some special challenges yourself.

The biggest challenge will be that you will soon discover you've married two people: your new spouse and their former partner. The former partner may be deceased or live a thousand miles away, but they will be there. They will be there, for example, on former anniversaries. They will be there when your partner recalls something they used to do or say. Trust us, a former spouse, no matter how distant, still roams the halls of your new home. So go into this marriage with your eyes open. Talk about it. Let your partner know it's okay to talk about. Get this fact out in the open, and as you explore it, learn what makes you uncomfortable and what doesn't.

You may encounter the ghost of your partner's former spouse in a variety of places—in the kitchen, on vacations, and so on—but allow us to mention an area that is very personal: your love life. It is not uncommon for someone in your situation to have curiosities about your spouse's former lovemaking. This can be a difficult issue that festers for years if not exposed. Don't keep your concerns about this topic bottled up inside. Take our suggestion and, if this is a concern for you, talk about it when the two of you are relaxed and comfortable. Communication, as we will see in a later chapter, is the lifeblood of every healthy marriage. So practice it with this sensitive topic. Go slowly and listen to each other. The more you talk it through, the more at ease you will be with each other as you develop your own love life together. And see a competent counselor together if issues concerning a former spouse continue to haunt you.

IF YOU'RE BRINGING CHILDREN INTO A SECOND MARRIAGE

Stepfamily expert Ron L. Deal compares bringing children into a second marriage to trying to put together a 3-D jigsaw puzzle without a picture on the box cover to show what it's supposed to look like. Needless to say, it's complicated. But you already knew that, right?

We'll have much more to say on this topic in chapter 8, but for now, in this chapter devoted to exploring whether you are ready for remarriage, we simply want to ask you: Are your kids ready for your remarriage. Since you are in love and looking toward a future with a new spouse, you may need to take special care to be sure your children feel included and that they are part of this major decision that impacts their life—whether they are toddlers or in their twenties. When a mom or dad gets married again, the children need to know that their thoughts and feelings about the marriage were taken into consideration. You can do this by simply asking how they feel about your marriage. Of course, once you ask, you must be willing to listen. Whatever their response, do your best to let them know they are understood, regardless of their opinion. Reflect back their feelings. You might say, for example, "It sounds like you're really nervous about what our future will be like." Don't try to change opinions or solve problems. A warm, empathic conversation lets them know you take their feelings seriously. Be aware that they may have especially strong feelings about their other biological parent. They may even try to make you feel guilty about getting married again. That's when it is particularly important not to be judgmental. Of course if you have a child who is completely against your remarriage, you may want to consider seeing a counselor together who can help you process the issues more objectively.

A FINAL THOUGHT

Whatever your status—divorced, widowed, or neither—allow us to leave you with one final thought. Perhaps it is best posed as a question: What do you believe your chances of marital success are the second time around?

A recent study published in the *Journal of Family Psychology* revealed that most couples tend to be overly optimistic about their chances of marital success. Despite their awareness of the national divorce rate, couples dramatically underestimate their chances of a future divorce. On average, they peg their likelihood of divorce at about 10 percent, substantially below the national divorce likelihood of near 50 or 60 percent. Interestingly, these same couples estimated other people's likelihood to divorce much higher. The researchers concluded that "it is rather remarkable that so many people would think that there is no possibility that their marriage will end in divorce when half or more of all marriages are terminated in divorce." They go on to say that their findings support the view that "positive illusions about marriage appear to be more powerful than illusions about other aspects of life."[9] For this very reason we turn our attention in the next chapter to the myths of remarriage.

SYMBIS Report Page 7A
What's Your Remarriage Readiness?

So what's motivating you to get married, and is there anything about your personal context and history that you need to be aware of so that you give your marriage every advantage possible?

If you're using the SYMBIS Assessment, you'll discover a personalized snapshot of your motivation for remarriage as well as your remarriage readiness.

You can find the assessment at SYMBISassessment.com.

FOR REFLECTION

1. It's no secret that many couples (even those entering a second marriage) spend more time preparing for a wedding than they do preparing for their marriage. Since you are studying this book, you obviously are trying to avoid that trap. Why? What do you expect or hope to get out of this process of preparation?

2. Review the list of reasons people shouldn't get remarried (financial gain, to avoid loneliness, and so on). If you had to choose one of these reasons as one to which you are most prone, which one would it be and why?

3. We mentioned the idea that people need to fall in love for all the right reasons. What does this mean to you? What are the reasons you've fallen in love?

4. One of the personal marks of remarriage readiness is a sense of independence from your former spouse. Do you agree? And if so, how would you rate your independence, with 1 being total dependence and 10 being full independence? Can you identify one specific thing you can do right now to make this rating better?

5. When it comes to "relational readiness" for remarriage, we said similarities were crucial. What are the most important similarities you have with your partner? And what one dissimilarity between the two of you holds the most potential for causing problems?

6. Whether you are divorced, widowed, or marrying someone in one of those two categories, what do you think is one of the specific challenges you will personally face in this marriage because of that status? In other words, what challenge is unique to you in your new marriage, in comparison to the challenges faced by your new spouse?

HAVE YOU FACED THE MYTHS OF REMARRIAGE WITH HONESTY?

We have been poisoned by fairy tales.

Anais Nin

"This is the second time around for me," Rick confessed. He was considering asking the woman he'd been dating for several months to marry him and decided to see us in our counseling office before popping the question. We affirmed him for seeking objective help before making such a serious decision. Then he posed his primary question: "How can I avoid the same mistakes and problems that occurred in my last marriage?"

We weren't surprised by his question. We've heard it countless times. But we were taken aback by Rick's sincerity. Most people who ask the question do so rather flippantly, as if they already know the answer. And their answer, more often than not, is: "I won't have the same problems because I'm marrying a different person this time." But not Rick. He knew this was an illusion. A myth. In fact, it is one of the most common misbeliefs that remarrying persons swallow. So he wasn't about to even take a nibble. And we have a feeling you are the same way. You wouldn't be reading this book if you didn't have at least an inkling that remarriage is faced with just as many, if not more, misbeliefs than a first-time marriage. You've probably known remarried couples who swallowed the happily-ever-after pill and ended up feeling queasy. Why? Because just like those who married for the first time, they expected their relationship to be a fairy tale.

The belief in a happily-ever-after marriage is one of the most widely held and destructive marriage myths — even for second marriages. But it is only the tip of the marital-myth iceberg. Every difficult marriage is plagued by a vast assortment of misconceptions about what marriage should be.[1] In this chapter, we consider those ideas that are most harmful and most common to couples where one or both individuals are marrying for the second time:

> "And they lived happily ever after" is one of the most tragic sentences in literature. It's tragic because it's a falsehood. It is a myth that has led generations to expect something from marriage that is not possible.
>
> Joshua Liebman

1. "We expect exactly the same things from marriage."
2. "Everything good in our relationship will get better."
3. "Everything bad in my life will disappear."
4. "Adjustment to married life occurs more quickly in remarriage."
5. "My spouse will make me whole."

The goal of this chapter is to take the mythology out of marriage. For too long, marriage has been saddled with unrealistic expectations and misguided assumptions. Liberated from these five myths, couples can settle into the real world of marriage — with all its joys and sorrows, passion and pain.

MYTH ONE:
"WE EXPECT EXACTLY THE SAME THINGS FROM MARRIAGE"

What we anticipate seldom occurs; what we least expect generally happens—especially in marriage. Saying "I do" brings with it a host of conscious and unconscious expectations that aren't always fulfilled.

James and Emily, a couple in their early forties and married for two years, each had a clear image of what life together would be like, but they had never discussed their ideas. They, like most remarried newlyweds, simply assumed the other had an identical picture of marriage in mind. Nothing, however, could have been further from the truth.

Emily, who had been through a divorce and brought two children into this second marriage to James, put it this way. "I expected married life to bring more stability and predictability to our lifestyle. To me it meant working in the garden together and being with the kids around the house."

James, who had been a bachelor until now, had a different picture: "I wanted our marriage to be exciting and spontaneous, not a ho-hum routine like so many couples I've seen. To me it meant working out at the gym together and riding my motorcycle on the weekends."

As far back as early childhood, James and Emily began dreaming of how married life would be. They grew up in homes where parents modeled married life. They read books describing loving relationships. They watched television shows and movies depicting scenes from marriage. For years they had fantasized about life after crossing the threshold. Not only that, but Emily had reshaped her picture of what married life was about after going through a painful divorce. With little effort, each had formed an idea of what it would and should be like to live as a married couple.

Consciously and unconsciously, James and Emily painted brushstrokes on their mental marital canvases. But it never occurred to either of them that the other might be working from a different palette. They simply *assumed* their lifelong partner would work with complementary colors and in a similar style.

The first year of marriage, however, revealed sharp and unexpected contrasts. What Emily thought of as security, James thought of as boring. They valued many of the same things, but with different levels of intensity. Emily painted carefully with delicate pastels; James painted boldly with primary colors.

Most incongruous expectations fall into two major categories: unspoken rules and unconscious roles. Bringing both of them out into the open can save years of wear and tear on a new marriage.

SYMBIS Report Page 3
What Are Your Marriage Mindsets?

Every person brings a mindset to marriage — what you are saying, thinking, and believing when it comes to tying the knot. It's your attitude toward marriage, in general. Recent research reveals that you have one of five specific mindsets: Resolute, Rational, Romantic, Restless, and Reluctant.

If you're using the SYMBIS Assessment, you'll discover each of your individual marriage mindsets — and most importantly, how they mesh — in your personalized report.

You can find the assessment at SYMBISassessment.com.

UNSPOKEN RULES

Everyone lives by a set of rules that is rarely spoken but always known. Needless to say, unspoken rules become more vocal when our spouse "breaks" them. This became painfully obvious for Mark and Sharon when they celebrated their first New Year's Eve as a married couple.

"Where do you want to go for the holiday?" Mark asked Sharon.

"What do you mean? I've always stayed in and we order out Chinese food," she responded.

That's when it dawned on her: This was how she and her first husband always celebrated New Year's Eve. Not only that, she grew up in a home where this was how New Year's Eve was celebrated. It was a tradition she enjoyed and expected to carry into her marriage with Mark. She never talked to him about it; she just assumed. Mark, on the other hand, always imagined ringing in the new year with a fun-filled night on the town. Needless to say, Sharon held an unspoken rule she never even knew existed until Mark wanted to break it. *My first husband never questioned this tradition, so why should Mark?* Sharon reasoned. Well, this reasoning got Sharon and Mark into one of their first big fights. And it could have been easily avoided had they taken some time to examine their unspoken rules.

Examining your unspoken rules is a good way to keep little problems from becoming big ones. These rules play as significant a role in your second marriage as they did in your first. Here is a sampling of the rules we have heard from other couples.

- Don't interrupt another's work.
- Don't ask for help unless you are desperate.
- Downplay your successes.
- Don't talk about money in public.
- Never call attention to yourself.
- Don't volunteer to help.
- Don't work too long or too hard.
- Don't get sick.
- Never raise your voice.
- Don't talk about your body.
- Don't show up late.
- Clean the kitchen before you go to bed.

- Don't talk about your feelings.
- Don't drive fast.
- Never buy dessert at a restaurant.
- Don't be too serious about anything.
- Don't buy expensive gifts.

Workbook Exercise 3
Your Personal Ten Commandments

Are you walking through a marital minefield of unspoken rules? The exercise *Your Personal Ten Commandments* can help you heighten your awareness of your unspoken rules and thus avoid needless explosions. It will help you recognize that you are free to accept, reject, challenge, and change the rules for the sake of your relationship.

UNCONSCIOUS ROLES

The second source of mismatched expectations involves the unconscious roles that you and your partner fall into, almost involuntarily. Just as an actor in a dramatic performance follows a script, so do married couples. Without knowing it, a bride and groom are drawn into acting out roles that they form from a blend of their personal dispositions, family backgrounds, marital expectations, and—for those in a second marriage—the way they saw their first spouse behave.

Mark (married for the first time) and Jenny (married for the second time) ran into their unconscious roles head-on when they returned from their honeymoon and began to set up house, arranging furniture, organizing closets, and hanging pictures. Before they knew it, they were fighting. "Where do you want this table?" Mark asked.

"I don't know; where do you think it should go?" Jenny replied. "Just tell me where to put it!" Mark said, exasperated. Over and over again, they repeated this scenario, each one looking to the other to take the lead, but neither one doing so.

Unconsciously, Jenny and Mark were acting out the roles they had observed in their families of origin—and for Jenny a role that was reinforced in her first marriage. Jenny's dad, a fix-it kind of person with a decorator's eye, had all the right tools and was handy around the house. So was her first husband.

Mark's dad, on the other hand, was a busy executive who hardly knew how to replace a burned-out lightbulb, and his mom was the one who organized the home. And since he had not been married before as Jenny had, he took his cue about the role of a wife and the role of a husband from his parents. So both Mark and Jenny took on their "assigned" roles as husband and wife, then wondered why the other wasn't pulling his or her weight.

Of course, there are an endless number of unconscious roles husbands and wives fall into. Some of the more common ones include:

- the planner
- the navigator
- the shopper
- the money manager
- the secret-keeper
- the cook
- the comedian
- the gift-buyer
- the cleaner

If you are like most couples, you will try to follow a script that was written by the role models you grew up with—or by the script you wrote in a previous marriage. Being aware of this natural tendency is often all it takes to save you from a disappointing drama. Once you are aware of the roles you each tend to take, you can then discuss how to write a new script together.

Because of their prescribed roles, Mark and Jenny went through their first year of marriage without ever hanging a single picture! Not until they were in counseling did Mark and Jenny become aware of the reason for their stalemate and make a decision to change their unconsciously assigned roles. As Jenny said, "Writing our own script makes me feel like we are building our *own* marriage and not just being robots."

> Too many people miss the silver lining because they're expecting gold.
>
> Maurice Seitter

The expectations you bring to your partnership can make or break your marriage. Don't miss out on the sterling moments of marriage because your ideals are out of sync with your partner's. Don't believe the myth that you and your partner automatically come with the same expectations for marriage. Instead, remember that the more openly you discuss your differing expectations, the more likely you are to create a vision of marriage that you agree on—and that is unique to the two of you.

SYMBIS Report Page 7
What Are You Expecting?

Every person's expectations around who does what in their new marriage are shaped by the home they grew up in. And so many of the tasks we do in marriage are rarely discussed as a couple — we just fall into patterns of behavior without talking out about them — until our expectations about who does what don't align with our partner's expectations. That's why this page of the SYMBIS Report is incredibly insightful for so many couples. You'll find out instantly what each of you are expecting and how to get in sync more easily.

MYTH TWO:
"EVERYTHING GOOD IN OUR RELATIONSHIP WILL GET BETTER"

One need only listen to just about any top-forty song on the radio to hear the common but destructive myth that says everything good in a relationship will get better. The truth is that not *everything* gets better. Many things improve in relationships, but some things become more difficult. Every successful marriage requires necessary losses, and in choosing to marry, you inevitably go through a mourning process.

For starters, marriage sometimes means giving up a carefree lifestyle and coming to terms with new limits. It means unexpected inconveniences. And in a second marriage, it may mean trying to blend a family, cope with a difficult former spouse, deal with more than one set of in-laws, and so on.

Mike Mason, in his delightful book *The Mystery of Marriage*, likens marriage to a tree growing up through the center of one's living room. "It is something that is just there, and it is huge, and everything has been built around it, and wherever one happens to be going — to the fridge, to bed, to the bathroom, or out the front door — the tree has to be taken into account. It cannot be gone through; it must respectfully be gone around .... It is beautiful, unique, exotic: but also, let's face it, it is at times an enormous inconvenience."[2]

Workbook Exercise 4
Making Your Roles Conscious

Are you expecting a specific script to be played out in your marriage? Do you find your partner or yourself reading the wrong lines? To play your parts on a conscious level, take time to complete the exercise *Making Your Roles Conscious*. It may help you recast your parts and avoid a disenchanting drama.

Marriage is filled with both enjoyable and tedious tradeoffs, but by far the most dramatic loss experienced in a new marriage is the idealized image you have of your partner. This was the toughest myth we encountered in our marriage. Each of us had an airbrushed mental picture of who the other was. But eventually, married life asked us to look reality square in the face and reckon with the fact that we did not marry the person we thought we did. And—brace yourself—neither will you.

This belief is what petrifies many couples marrying for the second time. You believe that *this time I know the person I'm marrying,* and you do. But not as well as you thought. You never do. Why? Because at some level you're still holding on to this powerful myth.

All marriages begin with an emotional honeymoon, a time of deep and passionate romance. But this romance is inevitably temporary. In *The Road Less Traveled,* Dr. Scott Peck says that "no matter whom we fall in love with, we sooner or later fall out of love if the relationship continues long enough." He does not mean that we cease loving our partner. He means that the feeling of ecstatic love that characterizes the experience of falling in love always passes. "The honeymoon always ends," he states. "The bloom of romance always fades."[3]

> Love is an ideal thing, marriage a real thing; a confusion of the real with the ideal never goes unpunished.
>
> Johann Wolfgang von Goethe

It is an illusion that the romance in the beginning of a relationship will last forever. This may be hard to swallow (it was for us), but debunking the myth of eternal romance will do more than just about anything to help you build a lifelong happy marriage.

Here's the bottom line: Each of us constructs an idealized image of the person we marry. The image is planted by our partner's eager efforts to put his best foot forward,[4] but it takes root in the rich soil of our romantic fantasies. We *want* to see our partner at his best.

We imagine, for example, that he would never put on excess weight or become irritable with the children from our first marriage. We seek out and attend to what we find admirable and blank out every blemish. We see him as more noble, more attractive, more intelligent, more gifted than he really is. But not for long.

The stark fact is that this phase is necessarily fleeting. Some experts believe the half-life of romantic love is about three months, after which you have only half the amount of romantic feelings you started out with. Others believe romantic love stays at a peak for two to three years before starting to fade. Whichever theory is correct, you can be sure that the enchantment of romance will begin to fade eventually. The point is that we marry an image and only later discover the real person.

An attorney we know who handles many divorce cases told us that the number one reason two people split up is that they "refuse to accept the fact that they are married to a *human being.*"

In every marriage, mutual hope gives way to mutual disillusionment the moment you realize your partner is not the perfect person you thought you married.

> Love takes off masks that we fear we cannot live without and know we cannot live within.
>
> James Baldwin

But then again, he can't be. No human being can fulfill our idealized dreams. A letdown is inevitable. But there is sunshine behind the dark clouds of disappointment. Once you realize that your marriage is not a source of constant romance, you can appreciate the fleeting moments of romance for what they are—a very special experience.

Here's the good news: Disenchantment enables you to move into a deeper intimacy.

Workbook Exercise 5
From Idealizing to Realizing Your Partner

Once we accept the fact that all experiences of love do not conform to the ecstasy of romance, once we relinquish the hoped-for ideals of our partnership, we gain strength and discover the true beauty of marriage. The exercise *From Idealizing to Realizing Your Partner* can help you take the first steps in that direction.

MYTH THREE:
"EVERYTHING BAD IN MY LIFE WILL DISAPPEAR"

This myth has been handed down through countless generations, and its widespread appeal is epitomized in such storybook legends as *Cinderella*. In this story, a poor stepdaughter who toils as a servant for her wicked stepfamily is rescued by a handsome and gallant Prince Charming. They fall in love and "live happily ever after."

No matter that Cinderella has been socialized to feel at home among the kitchen ashes and would have no idea how to behave in the pomp and circumstance of the royal court. No matter that Prince Charming has grown up in an entirely different culture and acquired its education, tastes, and manners. No matter that the two of them know nothing about each other's attitudes toward the roles of wives and husbands. All they have in common is a glass slipper and a foot that fits it!

"Of course, love doesn't work that way," you say. "It's just a child's fable." That's true. But deep down, we long for a Prince Charming or Cinderella to right the wrongs and make everything bad go away—especially if this is our second marriage.

Many people marry to avoid or escape unpleasantness or to find financial security. But no matter how glorious the institution of marriage, it makes no guarantees. Marriage does not erase personal pain, insure financial security, or eliminate loneliness. Why? Because people get married primarily to further their own well-being, not to take care of their partner's needs. The bad traits and feelings you carried around before you were married remain with you as you leave the wedding chapel. A marriage certificate is not a magical glass slipper.

Marriage is, in actual fact, just a way of living. Before marriage, we don't expect life to be all sunshine and roses, but we seem to expect marriage to be that way. Psychiatrist John Levy, who counsels many married couples, writes that "people who have found everything disappointing are surprised and pained when marriage proves no exception. Most of the complaints about … matrimony arise not because it is worse than the rest of life, but because it is not incomparably better."[5]

Getting married cannot instantly cure all our ills, but marriage *can* become a powerful healing agent over time. If you are patient, marriage can help you overcome even some of the toughest of tribulations.

When three Colorado psychologists ran a marriage survey in the *Rocky Mountain News*, they were surprised by "the number of people who endured traumatic childhoods [as abused children or children of alcoholic or divorced parents] and healed themselves through good marriages." As one of the researchers explained it, "Good marriages overcome things we tend to think of as irretrievable losses or irreconcilable tragedies." In other words, there has been a major shift in focus from marriage therapy to *marriage as therapy*.

All of us, at least unconsciously, marry in the hope of healing our wounds. Even if we do not have a traumatic background, we still have hurts and unfilled needs that we carry inside. We all suffer from feelings of self-doubt, unworthiness, and inadequacy. No matter how nurturing our parents were, we never received enough attention and love. So in marriage we look to our spouse to convince us that we are worthwhile and to heal our infirmities—especially if we have a few bruises from a first marriage.[6]

In *Getting the Love You Want*, pastoral psychotherapist Harvell Hendrix explains that a healthy marriage becomes a place to wrap up unfinished business from childhood. The healing process begins gradually by uncovering and acknowledging our unresolved childhood issues. The healing continues through the years as we allow our spouses to love us and as we learn how to love them.

Prince Charles and Lady Diana most certainly had unmet hopes in their storybook romance. Few could have imagined the painful outcome years later. Robert Runcie, archbishop of Canterbury, however, must have had a hunch. He gave a marvelous homily at their wedding. In it he said, "Here is the stuff of which fairy tales are made, the prince and princess on their wedding day. But fairy tales usually end at this point with the simple phrase, 'They lived happily ever after.' This may be because fairy tales regard marriage as an anticlimax after the romance of courtship. This is not the Christian view. Our faith sees the wedding day not as a place of arrival but the place where the adventure begins."

Too bad the royal couple didn't act on Runcie's message. Too bad we, also, settle for myths and fairy tales when we could be living a real-life adventure.

> You don't marry one person; you marry three: The person you think they are, the person they are, and the person they are going to become as the result of being married to you.
>
> Richard Needham

Workbook Exercise 6
Exploring Unfinished Business

Marriage is not a cure-all for problems. But it can, with time, become an agent of healing, fostering psychological and spiritual growth. The exercise *Exploring Unfinished Business* will help you begin your healing journey together.

MYTH FOUR:
ADJUSTMENT TO MARRIED LIFE OCCURS MORE QUICKLY IN REMARRIAGE

If you are like the majority of remarrying people, you're optimistic. You're hopeful. You not only believe in marriage, you believe that because you have traveled this marriage pathway before, you will know how to adjust to it more quickly. After all, you have experienced the honeymoon phase the first time and, now wiser, know it truly is only a fleeting phase. Besides that, you are now more mature. Over the years you've become more self-aware than you were when you got married the first time. You may have more money now too, or at the very least, you've learned how to manage your money more effectively than when you were first starting out. You have a lot going for you this second time around. However, if you expect that once the wedding vows are spoken your new married life will settle into a comfortable groove, you're going to be doubly disappointed.

Karen, the mother of an eight-year-old daughter, was in her second marriage for nearly two years when we met her. "I keep waiting for our new family to settle down so we can all be happy, but it's not happening." She went on to tell us how much she had learned from her previous marriage that ended abruptly. "I never saw it coming, but after my husband left us, I did a lot of personal work. I'm a stronger person now." Then tears began to rim Karen's eyes, and she reached for a tissue. "That's why I'm so confused and frustrated. I thought life would be normal by now."

That was her mistake. Life in a new family is *not* normal. At least not for many years. Sure, if you're not bringing children into the marriage, that simplifies things, but if kids are part of the package, you can expect your period of adjustment to take quite a long time—so much so that we devote an entire chapter to this situation later in the book.

Even without children as part of the remarriage picture, however, you will have another complicating factor that extenuates the adjustment period: *baggage*. The proverbial baggage you bring into this current marriage from your previous one takes time to unpack.

Some call this the "invisible partner" of remarriage. He or she may live miles away, but on occasion it may seem like an ex-spouse is right there in your living room. Why? Because divorce does not completely sever all attachments between ex-spouses. And even if your first marriage did not end in divorce and you lost your loving partner in another tragedy, you will contend with his or her presence in your new marriage. Guaranteed. That's the price we pay for meaningful human relationships. After all, at one point you invested your entire being into this individual, but for whatever reason, the relationship is over. You can't expect to leave that unscathed. Eventually, you have to admit that you lost a part of yourself when that relationship died. And if you have never fully grieved that loss, you will have all the more baggage to contend with.

Here's how Hara Estroff Marano of *Psychology Today* put it: "One of the most helpful things someone who is contemplating remarriage or has recently remarried can do is to truly grieve the losses of the previous marriage—to see the goodness of the prior relationship as well as the negative aspects." She goes on to make this insightful point. "If couples explore the issues of the previous relationship together, it can contribute to the establishment of a strong foundation in the new relationship. Failure to do this exploration opens the door to projecting all kinds of baggage from the old relationship onto the new one."[7]

So don't be naive about remarriage. Know that no matter what your situation is, you do not have a shortcut to being fully adjusted and settled into a "normal" marriage anytime soon.

MYTH FIVE:
"MY SPOUSE WILL MAKE ME WHOLE"

The old saying "opposites attract" is based on the phenomenon that many individuals are drawn to people who complement them—who are good at things that they are not, who complete them in some way.

The book of Proverbs says, "As iron sharpens iron, so one person sharpens another."[8] Our incompleteness and differences give iron its roughness, its sharpening power. Marriage is a God-given way to improve and hone our beings. Marriage challenges us to new heights and calls us to be the best person possible, but neither marriage nor our partner will magically make us whole.

This myth usually begins with the belief that successful couples are "meant to be" and "made for each other." We have counseled numerous people who, having difficulties in their marriage, felt they had chosen the wrong person to marry. If only they had chosen "Mr. Right" or "Ms. Right," everything would have worked out. C'mon! It's ludicrous to believe that successful marriages depend on discovering the one person out of the more than four billion people on this earth who is just right for you. If you are single, the fact that there is no "one and only" does not mitigate careful screening of prospective spouses. But if you are married and are complaining because your marriage partner does not make you instantly "complete," that doesn't necessarily mean that you married the wrong person.

> The success of a marriage comes not in finding the "right" person, but in the ability of both partners to adjust to the real person they inevitably realize they married.
>
> John Fisher

Couples who swallow the myth that their spouse will make them whole become dependent on their partner in a way that is by all standards unhealthy. These couples cultivate what experts call an *enmeshed* relationship, characterized by a general reliance on their spouse for continual support, assurance, and wholeness. People who are in enmeshed relationships usually suffer from low self-esteem, and often they are easily controlled by their partner.

> Success in marriage does not come merely through finding the right mate, but through being the right mate.
>
> Barnett Brickner

Dependent partners desire happiness, not personal growth. They are not interested in nourishing the relationship but in being nourished by their partner. They believe the lie that says they will effortlessly be made whole simply by being married. And for those bringing kids into a second marriage, they may even believe that their new spouse will complete the picture for their children—that this new mommy or daddy will make their kids whole (more on that in a later chapter).

The opposite of an enmeshed marriage is a relationship of rugged self-reliance, often called the *disengaged* relationship. This term reflects the isolation and independence of spouses who are attempting to earn their sense of wholeness by relying on no one, even their marriage partner. This is an especially seductive tactic for people getting married for the second time. These people, too, are trying in vain to compensate for their feelings of inferiority.

SYMBIS Report Page 4
How's Your Wellbeing?

Your relationship can only be as healthy as the two of you. That's why exploring your wellbeing as individuals, as well as the wellbeing of your relationship, is vital to helping you successfully launch an enduring love together. It's one of the most important things you can do to "save your marriage before it starts."

If you're using the SYMBIS Assessment, you'll discover new insights about your wellbeing in your personalized report.

A sense of wholeness can never be achieved either in an enmeshed or in a disengaged relationship. Both are deeply flawed and dangerous. Instead, wholeness is found in an *interdependent* relationship, in which two people with self-respect and dignity make a commitment to nurture his or her own growth, as well as his or her partner's.

These relationships are also known as A-frame (dependent), H-frame (independent), and M-frame (interdependent) relationships.[9]

A H M

A-frame relationships are symbolized by the capital letter A. Partners have a strong couple identity but very little individual self-esteem. They think of themselves as a unit rather than as separate individuals. Like the long lines in the letter A, they lean on one another. The relationship is structured so that if one lets go, the other falls. And that is exactly what happens when one partner outgrows his or her dependency needs.

H-frame relationships are structured like a capital H. Partners stand virtually alone, each self-sufficient and neither influenced much by the other. There is little or no couple identity and little emotional connection. If one lets go, the other hardly feels a thing.

> If I am attached to another person because I cannot stand on my own two feet, he or she may be a life saver, but the relationship is not one of love.
>
> Erich Fromm

M-frame relationships rest on interdependence. Each partner has high self-esteem and is committed to helping the other partner grow. They could stand on their own, but they *choose* to be together. The relationship involves mutual influence and emotional support.

M-frame relationships exhibit a meaningful couple identity. If one lets go, the other feels a loss but recovers balance.

Like separate strings of a lute that quiver with the same music, there is beauty in a marriage that respects the individuality of its partners. In an interdependent marriage, joy is doubled, and sorrow is cut in half.

Workbook Exercise 7
Assessing Your Self-Image

Louis K. Anspacher said, "Marriage is that relation between man and woman in which the independence is equal, the dependence mutual, and the obligation reciprocal." The exercise *Assessing Your Self-Image* will help you construct an interdependent and fulfilling relationship.

A FINAL WORD ON MARITAL MYTHS

The goal of this chapter has been to help you dismantle five common and harmful marital myths: (1) "We expect exactly the same things from marriage," (2) "Everything good in our relationship will get better," (3) "Everything bad in my life will disappear," (4) "Adjustment to remarried life occurs more quickly in remarriage," and (5) "My spouse will make me whole." If you are discouraged by having held such fables as truth, take heart. Everyone enters marriage believing these falsehoods to some degree. And every successful marriage patiently works to challenge and debunk these myths.

> The bonds of matrimony are like any other bonds; they mature slowly.
>
> Peter DeVries

In biblical times, the special status of bride and groom lasted a full year. "If a man has recently married, he must not be sent to war or have any other duty laid on him. For one year he is to be free to stay at home and bring happiness to the wife he has married."[10] The beginning of marriage was a time of learning and adapting. It still is. So allow yourself the same luxury.

SYMBIS Report Page 5
Are You Getting the Love
and Support You Need?

Vital to your marriage and how your love grows is the social support you have around it. So why not take inventory of how nurturing your social network is and how friends and family are impacting your relationship? Being aware of how your two social worlds combine is an important part of building your love-life together.

If you're using the SYMBIS Assessment, you'll want to explore the social support you're receiving from both sides of the relationship. You'll also find it helpful to see how well you are doing at combining your two social worlds. This page of your personalized report will do exactly that.

FOR REFLECTION

1. With your partner, discuss the expectations you have of your life together. What unspoken values or expectations do each of you bring to your partnership? In what ways has a previous marriage shaped your expectations for your new marriage?

2. What three important things did you give up or will you have to give up to be married? Have you grieved that loss? What is the positive trade-off for you?

3. How do dating couples build façades? What did you do, intentionally or not, to create an unrealistically positive impression on your partner? When did disillusionment set in?

4. How important is "loving yourself" when it comes to loving your spouse? Is there a correlation?

5. What do you think of the idea that marriage can be a therapeutic, healing agent? In what areas in your life do you feel that you need healing? How could your spouse help you in those areas?

6. At what point does relational dependency become unhealthy? What about relational independence? How do you know whether or not you are experiencing interdependency in marriage?

7. Was your first marriage an A-, H-, or M-frame relationship? What specific lesson have you learned from the condition of your first marriage that can be applied to this new one? And what about your current relationship? Is it an A-, H-, or M-frame relationship?

A SPECIAL NOTE TO SYMBIS ASSESSMENT USERS

IF YOU ARE USING the SYMBIS Assessment with a certified SYMBIS Facilitator, we recommend reading the Appendix, "Discovering Your Personality Dynamics" (page 223) at this point. Why? Because the remaining chapters of *Saving Your Second Marriage Before It Starts* become all the more personal and applicable when you can look at each of the topics (love, communication, conflict, and all the rest) through the lens of your two personalities together.

SYMBIS Report Pages 8 and 9
Do You Know Your Personality Dynamics?

The greatest gift you will ever bring to each other in marriage is you. Your personalities are unique and God-given. That's why there has never been and never will be another marriage exactly like yours. And that's why the assessment helps you dig deep into your two personalities, shows how you fit together, and what you can do to leverage the differences in your personalities for lifelong love.

CAN YOU IDENTIFY YOUR LOVE STYLE?

*Love must be learned, and learned again
and again; there is no end to it.*
KATHERINE ANNE PORTER

When asked "What makes a good marriage?" the answer given by nearly 90 percent of the population is "Being in love."[1] When asked to list the essential ingredients of love as a basis for marriage, however, a survey of more than a thousand college students revealed that "no single item was mentioned by at least one half of those responding." In other words, we can't agree on what love is. Or perhaps more accurately, we don't *know* what love is. As one person in the survey said, "Love is like lightning—you may not know what it is, but you do know when it hits you."

Five hundred years ago, Chaucer said, "Love is blind." Maybe he was right, but for those entering marriage the second time around there's reason enough to strip off our blindfolds and look love square in the face. In this chapter we pose three critical questions: (1) What is love? (2) How does one give and receive love? and (3) How can you make love last a lifetime? We answer these questions by exploring the anatomy of love, its parts and pieces. Next we look at the unique styles of love each person brings to a marriage. We then explore the passages through which every couple must maneuver if they are to keep their love alive. We conclude with a point-by-point plan for making love last a lifetime.

THE ANATOMY OF LOVE

"What is love?" asked Shakespeare in *Twelfth Night*. The question has echoed for centuries, and there is still no definitive answer. Is love the *self-seeking* desire described by William Blake's poem: "Love seeketh only self to please"? Or is love the *self-sacrificial* stance described by the apostle Paul: "Love bears all things, believes all things, hopes all things, endures all things"?

Whatever love is, it is not easy to pin down, for love is a strange mixture of opposites. It includes affection and anger, excitement and boredom, stability and change, restriction and freedom. Love's ultimate paradox is two beings becoming one, yet remaining two.

We have found that love's paradoxical quality makes some couples question whether they are really in love. We meet dozens of engaged and married couples in this predicament every year. Scott and Courtney are an example. With their wedding date just three months away, Scott broke off their engagement because he wasn't sure he really loved Courtney. Cupid's arrow had seemingly lost its punch, and he was calling it quits.

"I have strong affection for Courtney," Scott confided, "but I'm not sure I have ever been in love with her. I don't even know what love is." Scott, like many others on the precipice of lifelong love, was uncertain and confused. "How do I know if it's true love or just a passing emotion?" he asked.

Wendy, another example, wondered about her love for Frederic. They had been married nearly four years, and love's intoxication had all but evaporated, or so it seemed. This was Frederic's second marriage. He lost his first wife to cancer. When Wendy agreed to marry him, she knew that meant becoming an instant mother to his two children. What she didn't know was how she'd feel after four years of marriage.

"At first I wanted to have a baby of our own, but Frederic insisted we wait," she told us. "Now that he's ready, I'm wondering if it is the right thing to do. I mean, how can I have a baby with Frederic when I don't even know if I still love him?" She paused for a moment, then said, "To be honest, it feels more like we are good friends managing a household together than good lovers enjoying each other's company. Is that what married love is supposed to feel like?"

Scott, facing marriage, and Wendy, launching into another year of marriage with her husband, both worried that love had slipped through their hands, or that they had never really held love at all. Both were struggling with the same question: What is love?

Workbook Exercise 8
Defining Love

We each have our own definition of love, even if we've never articulated it. The workbook exercise *Defining Love* will help you and your partner define more clearly what each of you means when you say, "I love you."

A few years ago, it was much more difficult to answer this question. For most of human history, love was the province of poets, philosophers, and sages. Social scientists would have nothing to do with it, believing that love was too mysterious and too intangible for scientific study.[2]

Fortunately, the study of love has become more respectable in recent years and is no longer taboo. Today, hundreds of studies and professional articles on love are being published each year. And there is much to be gleaned from this scientific harvest.

Robert Sternberg, a Yale University psychologist, has pioneered much of the new research. He developed the "triangular model" of love, one of the most encompassing views to date.[3] In his model, love, like a triangle, has three sides: *passion*, *intimacy*, and *commitment*.

PASSION

The *motivational* side of the triangle is passion, the spine-tingling sensation that moves us toward romance. Passion is sensual and sexual, characterized by physiological arousal and an intense desire for physical affection. Song of Songs, for example, celebrates the physical love between a man and woman in passion-filled poetry: "Let him kiss me with the kisses of his mouth — for your love is more delightful than wine."[4]

_____

The best proof of love is trust.

Joyce Brothers

_____

But passion can also be possessive, fostering a fascination that borders on obsession. It drives couples to an extreme level of preoccupation with one another, to the point where they can't bear to tear themselves apart. At this stage, other relationships aren't even considered.

Sternberg explains that at first couples experience a rapidly growing physical attraction, but after a while they incorporate the ecstasy of passion into the fuller picture of love. Pure passion is self-seeking until it is linked with intimacy.

INTIMACY

The *emotional* side of love's triangle is intimacy. Love without intimacy is only a hormonal illusion. One cannot desire another person over the long haul without really *knowing* that person.

Intimacy has a "best friend" or "soul mate" quality about it. We all want someone who knows us better than anyone else — and still accepts us. And we want someone who holds nothing back from us, someone who trusts us with personal secrets. Intimacy fills our heart's deepest longings for closeness and acceptance.

People who have successfully built an intimate relationship know its power and comfort, but they also know that taking the emotional risks that allow intimacy to happen isn't easy. Without careful nurturing, intimacy withers. In *Finding the Love of Your Life*, Neil Clark Warren identifies a lack of intimacy as the number one enemy of marriage. He goes on to say that if two people do not know each other deeply, they can never merge or bond, becoming what the Bible calls "one flesh." "Without intimacy," he says, "they will be isolated and alone—even while living under the same roof."[5]

The fulfillment of love hinges on closeness, sharing, communication, honesty, and support. As one heart given in exchange for another, marriage provides the deepest and most radical expression of intimacy.

COMMITMENT

The *cognitive* and willful side of the love triangle is commitment. Commitment looks toward a future that cannot be seen and promises to be there—until death. "Without being bound to the fulfillment of our promises," writes philosopher Hannah Arendt, "we would be condemned to wander helplessly in the darkness of each person's lonely heart."

Commitment creates a small island of certainty in the swirling waters of uncertainty. As the mooring of marriage, commitment secures love for our partner when passion burns low and when turbulent times and fierce impulses overtake us.

Commitment says, "I love you because you are you, not because of what you do or how I feel." The Swiss counselor Paul Tournier describes the marriage vow as a gift, "total, definite, unreserved ... a personal and unchangeable commitment."[6] The longevity of love and the health of a marriage depend mightily on the strength of commitment.

Passion, intimacy, and commitment are the hot, warm, and cold ingredients in love's recipe. And these ingredients vary, because the levels of intimacy, passion, and commitment change from time to time and from person to person. You can visualize the fluidity of love by considering how the love triangle changes in size and shape as the three components of love increase and decrease. The triangle's area represents the amount of love. Large amounts of intimacy, passion, and commitment yield a large triangle. The larger the triangle, the more love.

With Sternberg's help, we have come closer to discovering what love is, but a pressing question still remains: How is love given and received? To answer this question we will first study love styles, and then we will examine love's stages.

LOVE STYLES

Often we assume that love means to our partners what it means to us, but the truth is two people rarely mean the same thing when they say, "I love you." In marriage counseling, we hear again and again the sometimes plaintive, sometimes desperate words, "I just don't love her anymore" or "I love him, but I'm not *in* love with him." What this usually means is that a particular quality a person wants in love is missing or has changed.

Consider John and Monica, who came to see us for counseling after just fifteen months of marriage. In their first session, which brimmed with tension, they complained of "falling out of love" with each other.

"You hardly ever tell me that you love me," said Monica. She was fighting back tears as she looked at her husband.

"Of course I love you," John replied, "but I shouldn't have to tell you I love you—I *do* loving things for you. My actions speak louder than my words ever could."

Were Monica and John "out of love"? No. Their love styles were merely out of sync and causing insufferable tension. It is not uncommon for one partner, like John, to feel loving toward his spouse while the spouse feels unloved. But their love has not withered; it has simply taken on a style that is not meeting a partner's needs.

As the session with Monica and John continued, we discovered that the "loving things" John was doing for Monica included bringing home a paycheck, fixing broken appliances, and avoiding arguments.

"These are things any good husband would do routinely," said Monica. "They have nothing to do with what *I* call love." Monica defined love as using terms of endearment, giving gifts, touching, and showing tenderness—all of which made John uncomfortable, because they didn't fit into his idea of true love. According to John, what Monica wanted was the mere "fluffy stuff" of love.

> Looking back, I have this to regret, that too often when I loved, I did not say so.
>
> **David Grayson**

Both Monica and John were assuming that how they loved was how their partner wanted to be loved, and both were feeling unloved because of it. Neither was fully aware of, let alone adapting to, the other's differing love style.

When Elizabeth Barrett Browning asked "How do I love thee?" in one of her most famous sonnets, she probably never imagined that the answer would one day be studied with scientific precision.[7] But that is exactly what researchers like Robert Sternberg have attempted to do. His triangular model not only identifies love's parts and pieces;

it explains how partners like John and Monica give and receive love differently.

Sternberg's triangle can change shape depending on the varying degrees of passion, intimacy, and commitment in the relationship. A triangle with three equal sides represents what Sternberg calls a *consummate* love, in which all three components are equally matched. But when one leg of the triangle becomes longer than the others, a new kind of unbalanced love style emerges, either *romantic, foolish,* or *companionable.*

Romantic love, which relies on a combination of intimacy and passion, is physical attraction mixed with a deep sense of caring. But commitment takes a back seat in romantic love.

Foolish love results from a combination of passion and commitment. But this time, intimacy is mostly absent. It is foolish in the sense that a commitment is made on the basis of passion without the stabilizing element of intimate knowledge.

Companionable love evolves from a combination of intimacy and commitment with passion fading to the background. It is essentially a long-term, committed friendship. This occurs in marriage when physical attraction becomes less important than the security of knowing and being known by your partner.

Sometimes ill-fated marriages are built exclusively on either romantic love, foolish love, or companionable love. But successful marriages demand more—even when a romantic, foolish, or companionable love style becomes momentarily predominant.

Consummate love results from the full combination of love's three components: passion, intimacy, and commitment. Consummate love is the goal toward which every marriage strives, and most marriages achieve it, at least for a time. *Maintaining* consummate love, however, is where many marriages falter. Attaining consummate love is like meeting your target goal in a weight-loss program—reaching the goal is often easier than maintaining it. The attainment of consummate love is no guarantee that it will last indefinitely. It won't.

Marriage partners do not lock into consummate love once and for all, for love styles in marriage change. At times, for one spouse some elements become stronger than others, and a style of loving emerges that is not in step with the other partner's style. In John and Monica's case, John valued companionable love at that stage in their relationship, while Monica wanted romantic love. He needed a deeper sense of bonding and certainty, but his wife longed for more sensuality. They were meeting each other's intimacy needs but falling short on passion and commitment. For the time being they were out of step.

Going back to our examples at the beginning of the chapter, we can understand the problem with Scott and Courtney. Scott broke off his engagement with Courtney because he was caught up in a romantic style of love and felt uncertain about lifelong commitment. While intimacy and passion were alive and well, Scott feared his strong feelings of attraction might only be a fleeting phase. In an agonizing counseling session, he and Courtney decided not to break up, but to remain engaged and postpone their wedding. Four months later, after Scott had had time to cultivate commitment into his love style, they set a new wedding date and were married later that year.

Wendy and Frederic, who had been married for four years, also suffered from being out of sync in their styles of loving. Frederic's love was sturdy, supported by passion, intimacy, and commitment. But Wendy had lost that passionate feeling. Her companionable love style caused her to doubt her real love for Frederic and question whether she was wise to have a baby with him. However, after a long overdue romantic getaway with Frederic—where the kids stayed home with grandparents—and some deliberate actions to cultivate passion, Wendy's love style once again fell in sync with her husband's.

Such is the dance of love. Day in and day out we clumsily shuffle, stumble, and even step on one another's feet in our relationships. But that does not diminish the graceful moments when two partners finally experience the same rhythm of passion, intimacy, and commitment.

Anne Morrow Lindbergh wrote about the dance of love in her wonderful little book *Gift from the Sea*:

> When you love someone you do not love them all the time, in exactly the same way, from moment to moment. It is an impossibility. It is even a lie to pretend to. And yet this is exactly what

most of us demand. We have so little faith in the ebb and flow of life, of love, of relationships. We leap at the flow of the tide and resist in terror its ebb. We are afraid it will never return. We insist on permanency, on duration, on continuity; when the only continuity possible, in life as in love, is in growth, in fluidity—in freedom.[8]

ENSURING HOT MONOGAMY

Since we are talking about love over the life span, we want to paint a picture of the stages your love life is likely to go through. However, before we do so, we feel it's important in this chapter to first talk about sex. After all, you're thinking about it—and it's a good thing you are. Why? Because your brain is the most important sexual organ you have.

The human sex drive operates out of the "cortex," that thin outer layer of the brain where all learning takes place. Humans use their highly developed brains to learn how, when, where, and whether they will give expression to their sexual urges—this ability for control is what separates us from the animals.

So does this mean that having sex as a husband and wife does not involve "animal instincts"? Not on your life.

We recently spent an entire day, breakfast through dinner, with renowned sex therapists Clifford and Joyce Penner from Pasadena, California. The Penners, authors of *The Gift of Sex*, have been counseling people on sexual issues for nearly three decades and have heard every conceivable story you can imagine on the topic. They have devoted their professional lives to helping people enjoy sexuality to the fullest. They understand the mechanics of what makes sex good and why it sometimes goes painfully wrong.

So what did we learn from the Penners about getting your sex life off to a great start? First, you've got to realize that your spouse may not be interested in sex whenever you are. Sexual desire is not "contagious." If you are in the mood you can't expect that, by default, your spouse will be too. Think of your sex drive as an appetite. "Just as each of you will differ in your appetite for food," says Joyce Penner, "you will likely experience differences in your sexual appetites." The point is that you will have to learn to coordinate your sexual desires without "overfeeding" one of you.

Another important fact to keep in mind is that sex between a husband and wife need not be spontaneous. The movies make it seem like sex is always an exhilarating moment of passion that happens naturally, without planning. Any idea how much scripting and setup goes into making it seem that way? In reality, married couples don't necessarily wait for some mysterious erotic energy to grab them. As the Penners say, "Some of the most satisfying sexual encounters between you and your spouse will often be the ones you plan and talk about."

In fact, the more you talk about your sex life, the more likely it is to be fulfilling. That's why we've included an extensive workbook exercise on the topic.

Workbook Exercise 9
Getting Your Sex Life Off to a Great Start

"There is hardly anyone whose sexual life," said Somerset Maugham, "if it were broadcast, would not fill the world at large with surprise and horror." He may be right, but through this exercise, *Getting Your Sex Life Off to a Great Start*, we intend to help you minimize both while maximizing your love life.

WHAT ABOUT LIVING TOGETHER?

When we talk to engaged couples about increasing the odds of lifelong love, we often get a question about cohabitation. Not so long ago, it was called "shacking up" and it was rare, about 1 in 141 couples. Today, it's closer to two thirds of couples. To put it another way, in 1960, about 450,000 unmarried couples lived together.[9] Now the number is more than 7.8 million.[10] Why? Pragmatic reasons, such as sharing the bills, makes cohabiting appealing for some. And many believe it's one of the best ways to prepare for marriage.

In fact, the National Marriage Project at the University of Virginia, found that nearly half of twentysomethings agreed with the statement, "You would only marry someone if he or she agreed to live together with you first, so that you could find out whether you really get along." About two thirds said they believed that moving in together before marriage was a good way to avoid divorce.[11]

So does cohabiting lead to good marriages or the polar opposite—increasing the likelihood of divorce? Here's what we know: Couples who cohabit before marriage (and especially before an engagement) tend to be less satisfied with their marriages—and more likely to divorce—than couples who do not. These negative outcomes are called the cohabitation effect.

Researchers characterize this effect as "sliding, not deciding."[12] Moving from dating to sleeping over to sleeping over a lot to cohabitation can be a gradual slope, one not marked by rings or ceremonies or sometimes even a conversation. Couples bypass talking about why they want to live together and what it will mean.[13]

But the detrimental side of the cohabitation effect is about more than just "sliding." Psychologist Meg Jay, author of *The Defining Decade*, says it's due to "gender asymmetry."[14] Women tend to see cohabiting as a step toward marriage, while some men see it as a way to stall marriage. It is easy to see how such conflicted, often unconscious, motives could be unhealthy.

One thing men and women do agree on, however, is that their

standards for a live-in partner are lower than they are for a spouse.[15] Cohabiters want to feel committed to their partners, yet they are often confused about whether they have consciously chosen their mates. Founding relationships on convenience or ambiguity can interfere with the process of claiming the people we love. A life built on top of "maybe you'll do" simply does not feel as dedicated as a life built on top of the "we do" of marriage.

Perhaps that's why, long before all the research studies were conducted, Paul wrote, "Sex is a much spiritual mystery as physical fact. We must not pursue the kind of sex that avoids commitment and intimacy, leaving us more lonely than ever."[16]

If you're considering moving in together before you marry, or you're already doing so, it's a topic worthy of discussion with a trusted counselor, marriage mentor, or minister.

LOVE'S STAGES

Who, newly in love, preoccupied from morning till night with thoughts of love, can believe they will ever be out of step with their partner, that the feelings they are experiencing so strongly will ever fade? Certainly no bride or groom wants to hear that their flame will burn lower in time. But in a sense, it will. The passionate love that begins a marriage cannot sustain a marriage. Newlyweds who equate true love only with passion are doomed to disappointment.

The love you now have for your partner will undergo numerous changes and evolve into many different forms over a lifetime together. Accepting this fact can help you keep your love alive, saving your marriage before it starts. But more importantly, accepting love's changeable nature allows you to relax and enjoy its many manifestations. Over time, you will see how love's many forms strengthen and deepen your relationship, enriching your lives with its exquisite beauty and rare character.

Every marriage faces pressure points that test a couple's mettle:

getting adjusted to one another, launching a new career, the birth of the first child and subsequent children, children going to school and moving out of the house, serious illness, and retirement. Then add to this list the unique pressures that surround a remarriage—such as stepparenting, or an ex-spouse or two—and the testing of one's mettle becomes even tougher. These milestones and challenges can cause upheaval in the happiest of marriages. If change is not expected and planned for, love is thrown off course. But if the marriage is good and change is anticipated, there is a gradual process of acclimation, and love finds a new sense of fulfillment.

> Young love is a flame; very pretty, very hot and fierce, but still only light and flickering. The love of the older and disciplined heart is as coals, deep-burning, unquenchable.
>
> Henry Ward Beecher

Marriage is a journey through predictable passages, or stages, of love. These stages—romance, power struggle, cooperation, mutuality, and cocreativity—are sequential seasons of love in marriage. Each stage has its own challenges and opportunities, and each builds on each other, eventually bringing your love life to its full potential.[17]

STAGE ONE: ROMANCE

The initial stage of love in marriage is romance, a time when couples nearly forget that they are unique individuals with separate identities. In this stage of enchantment, the couple takes complete delight in each other. Reaching out to fulfill their deepest needs for intimacy, they experience a kind of mystical union, and they celebrate the ecstasy of bliss and belonging.

STAGE TWO: POWER STRUGGLE

This stage, rife with tension, begins when idiosyncrasies emerge and differences become glaring. Two independent persons forming a way of life together eventually run into power struggles and must learn to adjust to each other's ways. The intensity and turmoil of this stage varies among couples, but almost every couple engages in the struggle. And couples in a remarriage are especially susceptible to it. Successful passage through this stage, however, enables each partner to say, "Okay. So I am willing to admit that my romance with a perfect partner is an illusion. However, I am still fascinated with the mystery of who you are, and I am willing to pursue romance with you and journey together toward a more mature love."

STAGE THREE: COOPERATION

This stage is like a breath of fresh air for couples who have stayed the course and successfully navigated the perilous passage of power struggles. Now, a sense of acceptance and a willingness to change enters the relationship. For those with children from a previous marriage, the cooperation is especially evident when it comes to parenting issues. A new depth develops as more healthy ways of being together begin. Couples in this stage realize that love is not so much about looking *outward* at each other as it is about looking *inward* at themselves, taking responsibility for their own personal problems. In this stage, couples relinquish the illusion that their partner needs to make them happy, and they redefine love by coming to grips with fears and defenses, projections and hurts.

STAGE FOUR: MUTUALITY

While a monumental change began in Stage Three, it was still a time when old problems and fears reemerged, especially in stressful times. But as love grows, couples eventually enter a new stage, almost unexpectedly, where mutuality becomes the fundamental way of being together. It is a stage of feeling at one with each other, where each feels a secure sense of belonging. Just when couples are wondering if they would ever escape old, unhealthy patterns, they discover a new reality—and are surprised by the joy of mutual intimacy.

STAGE FIVE: COCREATIVITY

In Stage Four, the intimacy each couple yearns for and struggles to achieve is an experienced reality. But as partners become older, retire, and face the end of life together, they develop a more pronounced energy of cocreativity. The rhythm of intimacy comes to a new and final flourish. Love overflows. Secure in themselves and in their love, couples have an abundant flow of energy for action in the world at large. This profound and peaceful period of love transcends all previous stages and results in a stronger and deeper love than any other. In cocreativity, couples realize that they are not made just for each other; they are also called to a ministry of love to everyone and everything. Thus, the cocreative couple develops a web of meaningful interrelationships that support the marriage and deepen its joys. In this final stage, partners are able to say, "We have put a lot of miles on this marriage. It has been exasperating, elating, horrible, wonderful, shackling, freeing. It has been our single most intimate source of conflict and of joy. Still, it has so much to offer."

> You will find as you look back upon your life that the moments when you have truly lived are the moments when you have done things in the spirit of love.
>
> Henry Drummond

Over a life span, love changes. But it becomes no less intimate, no less meaningful, no less important. For in the measure that passion recedes, the vacancy is replaced with a deeper, more abiding sense of intimacy, care, and cocreativity. As the flame fades, deep-burning coals emerge.

MAKING LOVE LAST A LIFETIME

"There is hardly any enterprise which is started with such tremendous hopes and expectations, and yet, which fails so regularly, as love," said Erich Fromm. The title of his classic book, *The Art of Loving*, is a message in itself. Lifelong love does not happen by chance but is an art that must be learned, practiced, and honed.

Every successful marriage is the result of two people working diligently and skillfully to cultivate their love. When they combine passion, intimacy, and commitment, they are able to grow a flourishing, healthy marriage.

Here are a few tips for planting your own marital Eden.

CULTIVATE PASSION

"Whatever happened to romance and passion?" cried Kelli, whose Don Juan had suddenly turned into a couch potato. Before they were married, Kelli and Mike enjoyed romantic picnics and passion-filled kisses, sometimes even stealing a kiss while waiting at a traffic light. On occasion, Mike would surprise Kelli with a bouquet of flowers. And Kelli would often treat Mike to his favorite ice cream, peanut-butter chocolate.

Workbook Exercise 10
Your Changing Love Style

Understanding that love does not always consist of equal amounts of the same ingredients helps couples prepare for the changing styles of love over their life span. The workbook exercise *Your Changing Love Style* will help you and your partner explore how your love might develop.

"He was the ultimate romantic," said Kelli wistfully. "Now all he does is come home, pick up the remote control, and surf through the channels on television. Sometimes I think he finds the TV more interesting than I am."

The loss of passionate romance is a common complaint, whether couples have been married one year or twenty-five. It seems that once the confetti and rice are swept away and the last of the wedding cake is put in the freezer, so is the couple's passion.

It is unrealistic to expect the exhilarating peaks of passion to remain constant. But marriage in no way requires passion to be put on ice. Love grows less exciting with time for the same reasons that the second run on a fast toboggan slide is less exciting than the first. But as any long-term, happily married couple can tell you, the excitement may decrease, but the real pleasure can still increase.

> When love and skill work together, expect a masterpiece.
>
> John Ruskin

Science agrees. A study of both a group of high school seniors and a group of couples who had been married more than twenty years found that both groups had a more romantic, passionate view of love than couples who had been married less than five years.[18] The researchers concluded that high school students had not given up their romantic view of love, and the older couples were enjoying "boomerang passion" as a result of their long-term investment in tending their marriages.

What are the secrets of these thriving older couples? How do they rekindle the sometimes flickering flame of passion? Here are three of the strategies of happily married couples.[19]

Practice meaningful touch. Sex therapists have long known what successful married couples soon learn. Affection, in the form of touching, is not only a preliminary to making love; it is a language that speaks more eloquently than words. Sheldon Van Auken, writing about his marriage to Davy in the book *A Severe Mercy*, illustrates the profoundness of touch. "Davy had crept near to me still crouching and I put my arm about her, and she snuggled close. Neither of us spoke, not so much as a whispered word. We were together, we were close, we were overwhelmed by a great beauty. I know that it seemed to us both that we were completely one: we had no need to speak." Meaningful touch is the language of passion.

Plan mutually enjoyable experiences. Being married doesn't mean the fun has to end. Successful couples work diligently to associate their partners with positive experiences. Romantic dinners, trips to the theater, and vacations never stop being important to them. Passion plummets when a spouse begins to associate their partner primarily with dirty clothes thoughtlessly dropped on the floor, barked-out orders, crying, and nagging. Passion can only survive and thrive if the couple continues to "date" even after they marry.

Compliment your partner daily. The most important element of romantic passion for both husbands and wives is to feel special. Not only do they want to feel sexually attractive to their mates, but they want to know they are appreciated. Compliments feel good—both to give and to receive. So, to paraphrase a James Taylor song, "Shower the person you love with compliments."

When it comes to passion in marriage, the bottom line is that the intensity of early passion is only the beginning. We often illustrate it this way: A jet airliner from Seattle to New York uses 80 percent of its fuel in takeoff. A tremendous amount of energy is required to get the plane launched so it can reach a comfortable cruising altitude. The takeoff, however, is only the beginning. The cruise is the important part of the journey, and it requires a different kind of energy, one with more sustaining and even power. By cultivating a deep-rooted passion, you can avoid years of needless marital turbulence and enjoy soaring at altitudes never imagined.

CULTIVATE INTIMACY

Ideally, husbands and wives are best friends as well as lovers—sharing dreams, interests, fears, and hopes. But according to Stacey Oliker, a sociologist and marriage expert, the gap between true intimacy and real life remains wide. Only a small minority of couples experience genuine intimacy.[20]

How could this be? Oliker claims that marriage partners seek to fill this gap by being more intimate with close friends than they are with their mates. In *Best Friends and Marriage*, she states that many women, for example, seek out friends or relatives before confiding in their husbands. Similarly, when men were asked to name the person they would most likely talk to about their future dreams and ambitions, close friends outnumbered wives.[21]

Does this mean married people shouldn't have close friends? Absolutely not. But it does mean we need to take special care to cultivate intimacy in our marriages. Here are a few things to keep in mind.

Spend time together. One of the great illusions of our age is that love is self-sustaining. It is not. Marriage expert David Mace says, "Love must be fed and nurtured ... first and foremost it demands time." Studies indicate that marital happiness is highly correlated with the amount of time spent together. We often encourage busy couples to schedule lunches together or "no-television nights" at home. Heart-to-heart talks don't happen on the go.

Listen with a third ear. Studies on intimate sharing indicate that "not really listening" is the most fundamental error couples make. We

> When two people are under the influence of the most violent, most insane, most illusive, and most transient of passions, they are required to swear that they will remain in that excited, abnormal, and exhausting condition continuously until death do them part.
>
> George Bernard Shaw

have a tendency to interrupt our spouses or be impatient while they are telling a story. But intimacy is cultivated when we patiently listen—not only to the story, but also to the feelings our spouses are conveying. If you learn to do that, intimacy will blossom in your marriage. (We will discuss this in more detail in chapter 7.)

Practice unconditional acceptance. The deepest kind of sharing can take place only when there's no fear of rejection. Some married people walk on eggshells around their spouses, fearing that they might say or do something to upset them. One newly married woman told us she was afraid to cook when her husband was home because no matter how she prepared the food, he would find something to criticize about the way she was doing it. Nothing drains a relationship of intimacy faster than anxiety. And nothing promotes intimacy more than knowing you are unconditionally accepted, even though you aren't perfect.

> To be loved,
> be loveable.
>
> Ovid

Focus on commonalities. Intimacy grows when nurtured by shared emotions, experiences, and beliefs. Any couple who has been happily married for fifty years will tell you their differences: "He's always restless, I like to relax"; "He loves sweets, I like salty foods"; "He's a Democrat, I'm a Republican." But in spite of their differences, you will hear statements that reveal their commonalities. They usually begin with *we*: "We laugh at the same things"; "We love traveling in New England"; "We support an inner-city mission." The more couples focus on what they have in common, the deeper intimacy grows.

Explore spiritual terrain together. A lack of intimacy can often be traced to a lack of spiritual vitality. One study showed that spirituality ranked among the six most common characteristics of strong couples.[22] When two people have a spiritual hunger or spiritual awareness in common, they become soul mates. In other words, spirituality is the soul of marriage—without spiritual roots, couples are left with an emptiness and superficiality that prevent genuine intimacy. (We will have a more detailed discussion about this in chapter 9.)

Partners who do not cultivate intimacy will, at best, live in an "empty-shell" marriage. They will coordinate the practical details of their daily lives (who does the shopping, what car should be purchased), but they will live in an emotional and spiritual vacuum, never enjoying the full beauty of love.

Workbook Exercise 11
Cultivating Intimacy

The most satisfied married couples know each other's hearts. The workbook exercise *Cultivating Intimacy* will help you and your partner open your hearts and deepen your sense of intimacy.

CULTIVATE COMMITMENT

When Tevye, in *Fiddler on the Roof*, suddenly wants to know if his wife of twenty-five years loves him, he asks her point-blank, "Do you love me?" Their marriage had been arranged, and as Tevye explained to his wife, "My father and mother said we'd learn to love each other. And now I'm asking, Golde, do you love me?" Golde eventually says, "I suppose I do." To which Tevye replies, "After twenty-five years, it's nice to know." And it is. While the romantic rush of feelings will eventually fade, another kind of love, anchored in commitment, will take its place and bring stabilizing peace to your marriage.

> The hardest of all is learning to be a well of affection, and not a fountain; to show them we love them not when we feel like it, but when they do.
>
> Nan Fairbrother

To cultivate the important element of commitment in your new marriage, here are some pointers.

Assess the high value of commitment. I can't emphasize enough the importance of commitment in sustaining lifelong love. Three doctors who studied six thousand marriages and three thousand divorces concluded, "There may be nothing more important in a marriage than a determination that it shall persist. With such a determination, individuals force themselves to adjust and to accept situations which would seem sufficient grounds for a breakup, if continuation of the marriage were not the prime objective."[23] Commitment is the mortar that holds the stones of marriage in place.

> Chains do not hold a marriage together. It is threads, hundreds of tiny threads, which sew people together through the years.
>
> Robert Oxton Bolt

Meet your partner's needs. Everyone who has taken a general psychology class and studied Abraham Maslow's hierarchy can tell you that human beings have a fundamental need for security. One of the best ways to give people security is by meeting as many of their day-to-day needs as you can. For example, once partners meet each other's need to unwind after work, or the need to have one night out a week, the level of security in the relationship rises. Meeting even the smallest of needs can cultivate the security of commitment.

Honor your partner's promise. People can become so focused on their own commitment and the sacrifices they are making for their marriage that they miss the beauty of their spouse's promise to them. We counseled a young man in his first year of marriage who saw commitment keeping as a sucker's game—a moral scam to cheat him out of his last chance for happiness. Since his marriage wasn't as satisfying as he wanted, he was ready to cut bait and move on, even though his wife was desperately devoted to him. Until we pointed it out, he hadn't even considered her gift of commitment to him. But recognizing how faithful she was in honoring her vow of love, this young husband decided he too could aspire to the fine art of promise keeping. Honoring our spouse's promise is a good way to cultivate commitment.

Make your commitment part of your being. In a scene from Robert Bolt's play *A Man for All Seasons*, Thomas More explains to his daughter Margaret why he cannot go back on an oath he took. "When a man makes a promise, Meg, he puts himself into his own hands, like water. And if he opens his fingers to let it out, he need not hope to find himself again." As human beings, we create and define ourselves through commitments, and those commitments become an integral part of our identity. When we contradict our commitments, we lose ourselves and suffer an identity crisis. You can strengthen your commitment to your partner by choosing to make it a vital part of your being, by giving it top priority, so much so that to break it is to break who you are.

SYMBIS Report Page 10
How Are You Hardwired for Love?

Chances are that the two of you define love differently. Why? Because you have different personalities. And that means that once you're married you'll tend to give and receive love from your own perspective.

If you're using the SYMBIS Assessment, you'll discover exactly what you are each wanting from the other when it comes to sex and romance. Your personalized report will reveal exactly that.

Every thriving marriage is grounded in passion, intimacy, and commitment. Cultivating these three elements will help you successfully navigate the stages of love and make it last a lifetime.

FOR REFLECTION

1. When did you first say "I love you" to your partner? Recount the experience. What were you thinking and feeling?

2. In your love life right now, which component of love seems most powerful: passion, intimacy, or commitment? Why?

3. Why is it important to know that love takes different shapes over our life span? How has your love style been changed by a previous marriage? If you are bringing children into your second marriage, how might that impact your love style?

4. Passion is typically the first component of love to fade in marriage. What can you do to prepare for the inevitable fading of passion without letting it die out completely?

5. What do you do in your relationship to cultivate intimacy? What else can you do to cultivate intimacy, especially when you are busy?

6. Commitment is the bedrock of lasting love, giving security and allowing us to relax. Do you think there are times in marriage when commitment runs thin? If so, when and what can be done to prevent it?

7. How has your concept of love changed as a result of reading this chapter?

8. After reading this chapter, can you list some specific things you can do to make love last?

HAVE YOU DEVELOPED THE HABIT OF HAPPINESS?

Happiness is a habit — cultivate it.
ELBERT HUBBARD

We had just finished speaking at a retreat in the San Juan Islands when a plane that was to take us to another engagement buzzed overhead and landed on a nearby airstrip. Five minutes later we boarded the three-person, rickety-looking Cessna.

The pilot greeted us. "It's gonna be a little noisy up there," he said, "but it's a short hop back to Seattle and a real beauty this time of the evening."

We looked at each other, silently communicating our mutual fear about traveling in such a tiny aircraft. "Great!" Leslie managed to reply.

We secured our belts and headphones as the pilot started the engine. In no time at all we were barreling down the grass runway, three deer scattering into the woods before us. Forgetting our fear, we leaned close to the windows, watching a small rim of sunlight glisten off the snowy peaks of the Cascade Mountains. It was truly glorious.

We crossed over the islands of Puget Sound and approached the lights of a local airport. "The most important thing about landing is the attitude of the plane," said the pilot.

"You mean altitude, don't you?" I asked.

"No," the pilot explained. "The attitude has to do with the nose of the plane. If the attitude is too high, the plane will come down with a severe bounce. And if the attitude is too low, the plane may go out of control because of excessive landing speed."

Then the pilot said something that got our attention: *"The trick is to get the right attitude in spite of atmospheric conditions."*

Without knowing it, our pilot had given us a perfect analogy for creating a happy marriage — the trick is to develop the right attitude in spite of the circumstances we find ourselves in.

> Happiness seems made to be shared.
>
> Corneille

It is no accident that some couples who encounter marital turbulence navigate it successfully, while others in similar circumstances are buffeted by frustration, disappointment, and eventual despair. It is also no accident that some couples are radiant, positive, and happy, while other couples are beaten down, defeated, and anxiety ridden. Researchers who have searched for the difference between the two groups have come up with all kinds of explanations for marital success (long courtships, similar backgrounds, supportive families, good communication, well educated, and so on). But the bottom line is that happy couples *decide* to be happy. In spite of the troubles life deals them, they make happiness a habit.

As a couple, we have taught courses and seminars on marriage for a number of years, and we have at least two dozen of the latest academic textbooks on marriage and family in our personal library. One of our favorite textbooks, considered a classic by many, has in it an italicized sentence that bears repeating: *"The most important characteristic of a marriageable person is the habit of happiness."*[1]

In this chapter we focus more on you than on your marriage. For it is *your* attitude that will determine whether you and your partner "live happily ever after." We begin by exploring how you can literally program your mind for marital happiness. Next, we highlight two basic attitudes that can make or break your marriage. Then we uncover some of the most common saboteurs of a happy marriage, and we reveal the surprising secret of happy couples. Finally, we consider whether two people really can live "happily ever after."

PROGRAMMING YOUR MIND
FOR A HAPPY MARRIAGE

Happiness in marriage has nothing to do with luck and everything to do with will. I learned that the hard way.

During our first years of marriage, Leslie and I attended graduate school and lived in a small apartment complex with several other student couples. A few doors down from us lived Bob and Jessica, who had also recently married and moved to Los Angeles. We had a lot in common, except for one thing—they seemed to get all the breaks.

Their apartment was a corner unit and nicely furnished. We, on the other hand, lived with hand-me-down furnishings that included a bright yellow upholstered chair with worn-through arms and a faded rust-colored love seat covered in corduroy. Jessica worked in a posh department store and received substantial discounts that kept them in the latest fashions. We were still wearing the same clothes we had in college. I yearned for a teaching or research assistantship at school, while special opportunities like these seemed to fall into Bob's lap without his even trying. To top it all off, Bob and Jessica drove a brand new, bright red sports car given to them by their wealthy parents. In the apartment garage it sat next to our old gray Ford pickup. Like I said, they seemed to get all the breaks.

> If one thinks that one is happy, that is enough to be happy.
>
> Mme. De La Fayette

I became unhappy every time I looked at their new car. Here I was sweating it out in an old gray pickup without air conditioning, while they were enjoying their climate-controlled vehicle and their plush leather seats. It really began to depress me. I remember saying to myself, *Why do other people get all the breaks? Why do other people have it so easy?* To add insult to injury, I found myself becoming increasingly negative toward Leslie. Little things she did began to annoy me, or more accurately, I began to *allow* little things she did to annoy me. My self-pity was creating a negative mindset that began to color even my marriage.

After stewing for months about our meager salary and frugal lifestyle, and about how others seemed to have it easier than we did, a truth hit me in the most unlikely of places: a statistics course. In the midst of learning about cybernetics and multiple regressions, I sat down at the console of a computer and began to enter data. After forty-five minutes I finally got all the lines and columns in their proper places. I hit the panel with the palm of my hand and sat back in the swivel chair to watch it perform. But nothing happened. There was total and absolute silence. I was just getting ready to kick the machine when I looked up above regular eye-level to a white panel that was now illuminated. And there in simple numbers and plain English was the answer to my statistical problem.

I could not believe it. I thought the machine would cycle and recycle and flash multicolored lights as it analyzed the variables I had entered. But it had taken the computer only seven-hundredths of a second to give me my results.

I slumped in my chair, feeling inadequate, when my professor, Dr. Wallis, came along. "What's the trouble, Les?" he asked.

I told him how long it took me to put my problem into the computer and how it took only a millisecond for the computer to give me an answer. "How in the world can it do that?" I asked.

Dr. Wallis took my question seriously, telling me how a computer takes one iota of data and gives it a positive electrical impulse and stores it, or gives it a negative electrical impulse and stores it. After that, the computer simply recalls the information from its memory and combines it in new ways. Then he said, "It basically works like a human brain."

"What do you mean?" I asked.

"Our brains are programmed much like a computer. Just before we put any sound, sight, smell, taste, touch, or intuition into our mental computers, we stamp it as 'positive' or 'negative.' Then we store the sensation in our brains, and it permanently stays there. That's why you can't always remember a person's name, but you can always remember how you felt about them."

Knowing that I was more interested in psychology than cybernetics, Dr. Wallis added, "Unlike computers, however, humans develop a habit of programming their minds to be either mostly negative or mostly positive."

That's when it dawned on me: I was making myself and our marriage miserable, sitting around waiting for opportunity to come knocking and complaining because it wasn't. Without even knowing it, I had developed a bad habit of stamping my circumstances as "negative." Instead of making the best of our conditions, I was wallowing in self-pity and allowing them to get the best of me.

That afternoon in the computer lab was a turning point for me. From then on I determined to be happy. Not that I am always optimistic and on top of the world, but I now refuse to let my circumstances determine my mood — or my marriage. It all began by realizing just how destructive a negative attitude is to a person — and a partnership.

Workbook Exercise 12
Listening to Your Self-Talk

Learning to choose your attitude is not easy, but once mastered, a positive attitude paves the way for a fulfilling marriage. The workbook exercise *Listening to Your Self-Talk* will help you and your partner cultivate the habit of happiness.

THE POWER OF NEGATIVE THINKING

Most negative people feel they could be positive if they had a different job, lived in a better place, or married a different person. But happiness does not hinge on better circumstances. A person with bad attitudes will still be a person with bad attitudes, wherever and with whomever he or she lives.

By force of habit, each of us is either basically positive or basically negative. Our circumstances change with the weather, but our attitudes stay the same. The negative person defends his attitudes with the rationale of being realistic, while the positive person looks beyond the current state of affairs and sees people and situations in terms of possibilities.

Take Ron and Scott, both of them married about three years. They have good jobs, live in nice places, and attend the same church. Ron is basically a positive person. He puts things in their best light, allows his wife to be human, and does not judge everyone by a perfectionist standard. His life is not without disappointments and problems, but his problems do not keep him from being happily married.

Scott, on the other hand, is basically negative. He makes himself the judge and jury on every inevitable shortcoming in his marriage. His conversation is a negative commentary on life, and both he and his wife are ready to call it quits. Of course, Scott didn't start out that way. In the beginning he had what we call a "positive bias." In the honeymoon stage, everything his partner said or did was interpreted in a positive light, and she could do no wrong. But when the marriage ran into difficulties, as all marriages do, his disappointment and frustration caused Scott to shift to a negative bias, with the result that he saw everything his wife did in a negative light. She could now do no right!

Life was basically the same for Ron and Scott, so why the drastic difference in attitude? The problem for Scott arose not in his circumstances, but in how he interpreted them—even the most trivial situation was often seen in the worst possible light. While Ron would give his wife the benefit of the doubt if she didn't greet him warmly, for example, Scott would jump to negative conclusions: *She couldn't care less about me.* Ron's and Scott's realities were not that different—but their outlooks were.

Negative interpretations are guaranteed to sap the happiness out of marriage. But how do we cultivate positive attitudes when our spouses do something we dislike? The answer lies in *taking responsibility for our own feelings.*

I remember coming home one day flushed with excitement and eager to discuss some good news with Les. I can't remember the news now, but I remember his response: lukewarm enthusiasm. I wanted him to share my excitement, but for whatever reason, he didn't. "You upset me," I later told him. But the truth is, he didn't upset me. I upset myself. That sounds a little strange, but it's true. Before exploring why Les didn't join in my celebration, I jumped to a negative conclusion: *He doesn't even care that something good happened to me. He is only interested in himself.* Meanwhile, Les, who was feeling somewhat dejected that day because of a setback at work, was thinking, *She doesn't really care about me. She is only interested in herself.*

Since that time both of us have tried to adopt a "no fault, no blame" attitude. The idea is to suspend our negative evaluations about each other and remember that no one can *make* another person unhappy. Everyone is responsible for his or her own attitude.

Viktor Frankl, more than anyone else, exemplified the human ability to rise above circumstances and maintain a positive attitude. He was a twenty-six-year-old Jewish psychiatrist in Vienna, Austria, when he was arrested by Hitler's Gestapo and placed in a concentration camp. Month in and month out, he worked under the great smokestacks that belched out black carbon monoxide from the incinerators where his father, mother, sister, and wife had been cremated. Each day he hoped for a few slivers of carrots or peas in the daily bowl of soup. In cold weather, he got up an hour earlier than usual to wrap his feet and legs in scrap burlap and wire to shield them against the crippling cold of an East European winter.

When Viktor Frankl was finally called for inquisition, he stood naked in the center of a powerful white light, while men in shiny boots strode to and fro in the darkened shadows beyond the light. For hours they assailed him with questions and accusations, trying to break him down with every accusing lie they could think of. Already they had taken his wife, his family, his writing, his clothes, his wedding ring, and everything else of material value. But in the midst of this barrage of questions, an idea flashed across Frankl's mind: *They have taken from me everything I have — except the power to choose my own attitude.*

> What counts in making a happy marriage is not so much how compatible you are, but how you deal with incompatibility.
>
> **George Levinger**

Thankfully, most people are not required to cope with such devastating circumstances as the Jews faced in Nazi Germany. But the same principle that helped Viktor Frankl survive the death camps — choosing his own attitude — applies to every difficult circumstance wherever and whenever it occurs.

Millions of couples are robbed of happiness because one of the partners has developed a negative mind-set, blaming their unhappiness on things their spouse does or doesn't do. It's one of the worst mistakes a person can make in marriage. We often hear statements in counseling like "Her comments hurt me!" or "He makes me so angry." In reality, remarks and comments do not hurt or upset people; people can only upset themselves. Of course, being upset is a natural reaction to something we dislike, but that reaction can serve as a trigger for a more constructive, positive response.

When we recognize where the control resides — in ourselves and not in external events — we are able to reinterpret upsetting events and develop a positive attitude.

Workbook Exercise 13
Avoiding the Blame Game

Taking responsibility, not blaming others, is critical to solving unpleasant marriage scenarios. The workbook exercise *Avoiding the Blame Game* will help you and your partner take responsibility for your own attitudes and overcome tough times.

THE SECRET OF HAPPY COUPLES

What makes happy couples happy? Dr. Allen Parducci, a prominent UCLA researcher, asked this question and found that money, success, health, beauty, intelligence, or power have little to do with a couple's "subjective well-being" (lab-speak for happiness).[2] Instead, research reveals that the level of a couple's joy is determined by each partner's ability to *adjust to things beyond his or her control*.[3] Every happy couple has learned to find the right attitude in spite of the conditions they find themselves in.

Can you imagine for a moment how the Christmas story might have been written if Mary and Joseph had not had the capacity to adjust to things beyond their control? To begin with, Joseph had to adjust to the fact that Mary, his fiancée, was pregnant. According to Old Testament law, he could have had her stoned or sent her into some large distant city like Rome, Carthage, or Ephesus. Before he could break with her, however, God sent an angel to tell Joseph that Mary was with child by the Holy Spirit and would give birth to a Son whose name would be Jesus. So instead of sending Mary away, Joseph married her.[4]

While the first year of marriage is always difficult, Mary and Joseph faced a unique set of challenges. Nine months of pregnancy require enormous adjustments from a couple, regardless of how long they've been married—and this was no run-of-the-mill pregnancy. On top of dealing with the implications of the impending birth, Mary and Joseph were trying to establish their home, run a business, and learn how to live with each other seven days a week. Further, they were forced to close down their business and travel to Bethlehem as the first step of a Roman plan to raise taxes. Just what they needed!

Early one morning Mary and Joseph left their honeymoon abode behind them as they went out of the gate of Nazareth en route to Bethlehem. She was riding on the back of a little burro. (No easy ride. Some women can hardly ride in a Buick while they are waiting for the birth of a child, let alone on the back of a donkey!) Joseph had a short tether wrapped around his arm and anchored securely in his big fist to keep the little burro from dislodging Mary, who was more than eight months pregnant. At night they did not stop in a rooming house or motel as people might today. They stopped along the road, cooked with makeshift arrangements, slept on the hard ground, and made the best of a difficult situation.

> Treasure the love you receive above all. It will survive long after your good health has vanished.
>
> Og Mandino

Finally, when they arrived within sight of the city of Bethlehem, Mary stopped. She could not go another step. We can imagine her looking up at her husband and saying something like, "Joe, I cannot take another step. I am going to sit down here under this olive tree, and I want you to go into the city of Bethlehem and get us a room in the Bethlehem Hilton. I would like one in the front if possible so I can watch the crowds go up and down, and I will get room service and wait out the time for the baby to come."

Mary was a long way from home, worn out, tired, emotionally drained, and at the end of her rope. Furthermore, she must have wondered what she would do if her labor pains began and Joseph was not near. After all, her baby was almost due. Her anxiety level must have risen as she waited, watched, and eagerly scanned the highway for the familiar figure of Joseph. The teeming crowds moving along the highway paid her no attention.

Finally Joseph returned, his characteristic smile gone, his shoulders drooping. She listened as he told her his story. "Mary, I went to the hotel, but there was no room. It's filled with convention people. In fact, I went up and down the main street to every hotel and motel, but there are no rooms. Finally, I persuaded an old man to let us stay in the barn with his animals. He's charging an exorbitant price, Mary, but he promised me he would clean out the manure and cover the floor with fresh straw. And most of all, Mary, he said we could be alone, and he would not make us share the stall with any other couple."

Their hearts heavy, Mary and Joseph made their way to the stable, thankful at least for a shelter from the cold wind.

That night the Son of God was born.

Can you imagine how the Christmas story might have been written if Mary and Joseph had not had the capacity to adjust to things beyond their control?

Every couple on earth must learn to develop this capacity if they are to

> The good news is . . . the bad news can be turned into good news . . . when you change your attitude!
>
> Robert H. Schuller

enjoy a happy marriage. Life is filled with too many unexpected turns and unforeseen problems. You may not experience the challenges Mary and Joseph faced, but you will encounter your own unique set of difficulties. Without the capacity to rise above your circumstances, you will never cultivate happiness. And personally, we don't know how to do this unless it involves resting in the knowledge that God is ultimately in control. You may have more success, beauty, intelligence, health, and wealth than anyone else, but if you do not cultivate contentment in every circumstance, unhappiness is certain.

SABOTEURS OF A HAPPY MARRIAGE

In the previous section we showed you what happy couples do right. We would be remiss if we did not also show you the other side of marriage—what unhappy couples do wrong. If you are to cultivate the habit of happiness with your partner, you will need to avoid the poisons of self-pity, blame, and resentment.

Workbook Exercise 14
Adjusting to Things Beyond Your Control

Learning how to rise above difficult circumstances may be the greatest gift you can give your spouse. The workbook exercise *Adjusting to Things Beyond Your Control* will help you and your partner maintain a positive outlook when things appear gloomy.

SELF-PITY

Too many marriages have unknowingly missed out on happiness because of self-pity. Whether experienced by one partner or two, self-pity can bleed the joy out of a relationship. Even marriages that start out strong can be crippled and permanently damaged if self-pity is allowed to develop and run amok.

One afternoon we pulled into the driveway of some friends, who came from their house to greet us before we even got out of the car. They quickly passed the minimal civilities of the greeting and burst into a story of self-pity concerning their new pastorate.

"Our church is just awful," Rick complained. "They totally misrepresented themselves—we thought the congregation would be well-educated, like us, but it's blue collar! The previous pastor didn't do anything to help the church in the transition, and the people just don't appreciate us at all."

"And you should just see this house!" Jan said, gesturing at the cozy white two-story behind them. "It's so small we don't know what to do with half our stuff!"

The rest of the evening was no better. Rick and Jan reeled off one story after another to let us know how terrible their new circumstances were. And when one of them stepped out of the room, the other would tell us how worried he was about her, about how he coveted our prayers for their marriage. Self-pity had poisoned their entire lives.

> Joy is the serious business of heaven.
>
> C. S. Lewis

As we drove away from their home later that evening, we wondered what would happen to a couple so thoroughly consumed with self-pity.

We didn't have to wait long to see the results. Within a year Rick resigned from the church, and their marriage hit bottom. He and Jan tried to recover by moving to another city to start again, but Rick could not make it as a freelance preacher. The marriage crumbled.

The pain of self-pity that we inflict on ourselves often hurts friends and family too. So why do we continue to punish ourselves and others when the pain is not necessary? Hard times and bitter personal experiences are a part of every couple's life, and self-pity about those difficulties helps no one. In fact, no one can ever be an effective marriage partner with the added burden of self-pity to cope with. Self-pity is a luxury no happy marriage can afford.

BLAME

Ever since Adam blamed Eve, and Eve blamed the serpent, couples have employed the trick of finding excuses and shifting responsibility. A great deal of unhappiness in marriage can be traced to a mate's habitual tendency to blame his or her spouse.

For example, Stewart was in the middle of fixing a malfunctioning oven pilot light and could not find his screwdriver. He confronted

Christy, accusing her of misplacing it. "You never put my tools back in their place," he shouted. "You make me so upset."

"I didn't use your stupid screwdriver!" Christy replied. "Why do you always blame me for everything *you* do wrong?"

Voilà—another fight is born. Stewart often blamed Christy for things because she was an easy target. And by avoiding responsibility, Stewart was off the hook for the unhappiness in their home. Christy was to blame; *she* was the problem. Christy, in turn, fed the fire by taking offense at his false accusations. Instead of controlling her own attitude, she allowed her husband to control her responses.

In many unhappy relationships, one of the partners is a scapegoat, the one held responsible for the couple's unhappiness. The other partner sees him or her as the source of their difficulties. In effect, the blaming spouse is saying, "*You* are my problem." But he or she would be hard-pressed to find a marriage counselor who would agree. Professionals know better. They know that marital unhappiness is never caused by only one person. That's why therapists focus not on *who* is wrong, but on *what* is wrong.

Blaming almost always results in a marital blowup, as it did for Stewart and Christy. But through counseling, Stewart learned to own up to his emotions and curb his blaming. And when he didn't, Christy learned to avoid retaliation by directing her efforts toward solving the problem instead of having a confrontation.

Let's replay the situation, examining how Christy could change her response to Stewart's accusation:

Stewart: What happened to my screwdriver? You always take it and don't return it.

Christy: *(He's blaming me again. I feel like telling him, "I don't know what happened to your stupid screwdriver," but then we would have an argument that would leave both of us feeling bad. It would be better simply to focus on the problem.)* Wait a minute, when did you last use it?

Stewart: (distracted from his anger, he thinks about an answer) I haven't used it since last week.

Christy: Weren't you doing some work around the house last night?
Stewart: Oh, wait a minute—I guess I did use it last night.
Christy: Where did you use it?
Stewart: I don't know ... in the basement.
Christy: Why don't you look for it there?

As it happens, Stewart found the screwdriver in the basement, where he had used it the night before. By shifting into questioning rather than counterattacking, Christy was able to defuse a potential argument and find a solution to the problem.

Blame can be overcome, but if it is allowed to linger—if couples habitually play the blame game—their happiness quotient is inevitably depleted. Every symptomatic problem in marriage (apathy, irritation, boredom, anger, depression, etc.) can be traced to a breakdown in personal responsibility. If you are angry, it is not your husband's fault, but your own choice. If you are depressed, it is not because your wife is failing you, but because you have chosen to be depressed. The habit of blaming your spouse is completely contrary to the principle of taking responsibility for your own attitude.

> They can because they think they can.
>
> Virgil

RESENTMENT

No one is exempt from being treated unfairly. We can all justify the anger we feel about how a situation or someone (including our spouses or ex-spouses) unfairly complicated our existence. But when we hold on to our disappointment, pain, and anger, we only compound our troubles—for that is when resentment does its deadly work.

Resentment is like a cancer to relationships, at first small and imperceptible, but over time growing larger and spreading its poison through the entire relationship. When you ruminate about an injustice done to you, replaying it over and over again in your mind, it will trigger a flood of negative emotions that feed the hurt all the more.

Then comes a succession of confirming incidents to convince you that the object of your resentment is the source of all your unhappiness. There may be periods of remission when your mind is occupied with other challenges, but sooner or later you come back to times of brooding, and the cancer of resentment spreads like wildfire.

William could not let go of the harm his first wife had caused him. For no discernible reason, she left him and their two children after twelve years of marriage. In a counseling session with us, he said, "I keep thinking I'm over it, and then I get into another serious relationship and I'm reminded of all she did to ruin my life." We listened to William rattle off a laundry list of painful incidents until he had finally run his course. "Do you feel any better?" asked Les.

"About what?"

"About your current situation. You've spent nearly an hour telling us about the pain you carry from your first marriage, and I'm wondering if after recounting it again you feel any better."

"Not really," William replied.

And he never will. As we continue to replay the pain from the past we only deepen the cut of the initial wound. That's the danger of resentment.

Resentment, even if directed to someone other than a spouse, is always detrimental to marriage.[5] We have worked with many couples where one of the partners harbors resentment toward their parents — sometimes even years after their deaths.

Janice, thirty-one and once divorced, came to our office for counseling. We had hardly exchanged introductions when she abruptly poured out some of the most vitriolic words we had heard in a long time. "My father is the biggest hypocrite!" she exclaimed. "Sure, he gives more money to church than anyone else, but that's only because he *has* more money than anyone else. At home, though, he was the biggest jerk to my mom and me."

Janice went on to blame her father for every bad experience she had ever had, including her stormy three-year marriage that had ended in divorce. Her resentment toward her father had contributed to the breakdown of her marriage, but instead of seeing her resentment as the problem, she still focused the blame on her father. Even though her father was supporting her and her baby daughter and paying for her tuition to finish college, she blamed her dad for the mess she was in.

We worked with Janice over a few weeks. At one point I (Leslie) said, "Janice, I have a feeling that it is easier to blame your father and keep your resentment alive than it is to forgive him. If you forgive him, then the consequences for your actions would shift from him to you, and that's scary."

Eventually, Janice did make an honest effort to forgive her father, offering a prayer of forgiveness and taking responsibility for her own actions. She remarried, and although there was no miraculous or instantaneous change, she never went back to blaming her father for her problems.

A happy remarriage cannot survive the cancer of resentment. Like self-pity and blame, resentment eats at the human spirit and kills the capacity for joy. But if these toxins are removed, there is no reason a couple can't live happily ever after—or can they?

SYMBIS Report Page 11
How Do You Experience Each
Other When Stressed?

Marriage was never intended to make you happy — you make your marriage happy. How? It comes down to how each of you adjust to things beyond your control and manage stress.

If you're using the SYMBIS Assessment, you'll discover your personalized resiliency factors and learn how your partner is likely to experience your personality when you are feeling stressed or pressured. This can be invaluable when it comes to cultivating happiness together. Your personalized report will show you how.

CAN COUPLES REALLY LIVE HAPPILY EVER AFTER?

Every couple about to be married, whether they admit it or not, harbors dreams of a "perfect" life together. Many newlyweds have told us how "lucky" they felt on their wedding day to have met someone who understood them, who shared their likes and dislikes, and who was so compatible with them.

Yet, no matter how ideally suited they are, at some point every husband and wife realize that theirs is not a perfect match. They become aware that they do not always agree, that they do not think, feel, and behave in exactly the same manner, that merging their two personalities and preferences and backgrounds is much more difficult than they ever expected. Their bubble is burst, and they resign from the hope of living happily ever after.

But there is an alternative.

> God help the man who won't marry until he finds a perfect woman, and God help him still more if he finds her.
>
> Benjamin Tillett

Marriages can never be perfect because people are not perfect. Being human, every bride and groom has faults as well as virtues. We are at times gloomy, cranky, selfish, or unreasonable. We are a mixture of generous, altruistic feelings combined with self-seeking aims, petty vanities, and ambitions. We unite love and courage with selfishness and fear. Marriage is an alloy of gold and tin. If we expect more than this, we are doomed to disappointment.

So, how can a couple live happily ever after? Not by depending on externals. Too many couples view marriage as winning the lottery: They got lucky, and now they will have interesting and exciting experiences. Now they will be loved and affirmed. Now they will be fulfilled. But marriage is not like winning the lottery—at least not like we *think* winning the lottery would be. An unexpected cash windfall would certainly make you happy. But only for a short while.

Researchers have discovered that a random event (being "lucky") occurring without your input does not create long-term happiness. You need a sense of mastery, of control; you need the feeling that something good has happened because you *caused* it to happen.[6]

Living happily ever after only works when you *make* it work. When you take the raw materials of marriage—the good and the bad that you've brought together as persons—to design, create, and build a lasting bond, the result is an enduring and meaningful sense of genuine fulfillment. If, on the other hand, you are counting on the magic of marriage to make you happy, the relationship will leave you crushed, lonely, feeling like a failure, and resigned to your despair.

The habit of happiness is an inside job. If you find the right attitude in spite of atmospheric conditions, if you program your mind with positive impulses, and if you adjust to things beyond your control, you will discover that living happily ever after need not be a myth.

FOR REFLECTION

1. In recent years, more and more people have come to view happiness as the major purpose of marriage. What do you think? Has your opinion changed since your first marriage?

2. Part of your vows say something like "to love and to cherish your partner in sickness and in health." How can a person cultivate the habit of happiness even when things are not going well? Do you have examples of how you did or didn't do this in your first marriage?

3. Can you think of some examples from your own life where you rose above your difficult circumstances and *chose* to be happy? What keeps you from doing this sometimes?

4. In one survey after another, researchers have found that people who rate their marriage as "very happy" also rate life as a whole as "very happy." In your mind, what does this have to say about cultivating the habit of happiness?

5. While the culture into which we are born and our family background significantly influence our attitudes, each of us is ultimately responsible for how we choose to cope with life. On a scale of 1 – 10, how strongly do you agree with that statement?

CAN YOU SAY WHAT YOU MEAN AND UNDERSTAND WHAT YOU HEAR?

It is terrible to speak well and be wrong.

SOPHOCLES

Well, what do you think?" Leslie was standing in the middle of our tiny apartment twirling around to display her new dress. We had been married less than a week.

"It's good," I responded. "Are you ready to go? I'm starving."

"Good—I'm starving? That's all you can say?" Leslie didn't have to ask this rhetorical question. I could read it all over her face.

"Is something wrong?" I asked (my keen diagnostic sense was just budding).

"No."

"Well, let's go then."

"Wait, I'm going to change," Leslie said.

"Why? You look fine!"

Five minutes later I could hear weeping coming from the bedroom. *That's strange*, I thought. I walked to the door and opened it; the light was off. Leslie was curled up on the edge of the bed crying.

"What happened?" I exclaimed.

"Nothing."

"Are you all right?"

"Yes."

"Then why are you crying?"

No response.

In the silence both of us wondered what had just happened. I was bewildered. Leslie was hurt. But why?

This small incident during the first week of our marriage was the prime indicator that we did not speak the same language—or so it seemed.

Couples report that the number one problem they face in marriage is "a breakdown in communication." And with good reason. Whether a marriage sinks or swims depends on how well partners send and receive messages, how well they say what they mean and understand what they hear. Communication can either buoy relational intimacy or be the dead weight leading to its demise.

The best time to build communication skills, by the way, is when things are going well—in the very earliest stages of marriage. Research measuring how well engaged couples communicate compared to how well they communicate six years into their marriage shows that by learning effective skills early on they greatly increase their chances for success in marriage.[1] And that means that for the person who is entering a second marriage, his or her communication skills need to be closely examined (to determine whether they are effective or not), since they may already be somewhat entrenched from patterns established in the first marriage. At any rate, a few simple principles, thoroughly understood and regularly practiced, will make the difference between whether you sink or swim as a couple.

The purpose of this chapter is to help you become more understanding and better understood. We begin by underscoring the importance of learning to communicate. Next, we talk about the common causes of communication failure, and we reveal the bedrock of effective communication. We wrap up the chapter with a few of the most effective and proven communication rules of marriage.

SYMBIS Report Page 12
What Are Your Talk Styles?

Few things can influence how the two of you communicate more than your two personalities. Learning helpful techniques and communication strategies will be a huge boost — but better than that is uncovering how you are each hardwired for a great conversation.

If you're using the SYMBIS Assessment, you'll discover how your personalities can be leveraged to have the best conversations possible. Your personalized report will show you how and provide you with a custom plan for improvement.

WHY LEARN TO COMMUNICATE?

Time and again, we have seen faulty communication lines pull down an otherwise sturdy marriage: Both partners struggle to convey what they want or need in the relationship, never realizing they are speaking a language the other does not comprehend. Over the disappointment, the partners erect defenses against each other, becoming guarded. They stop confiding in each other, wall off parts of themselves, and withdraw emotionally from the relationship. They can't talk without blaming, so they stop listening. One spouse might leave, but if both stay they live together in an emotional divorce.

> There is no greater lie than a truth misunderstood.
>
> **William James**

I can't emphasize enough the importance of communication in marriage. In a revealing poll, almost all (97 percent) who rate their communication with their partner as excellent are happily married, compared to only 56 percent who rate their communication as poor. The poll concluded: "In an era of increasingly fragile marriages, a couple's ability to communicate is the single most important contributor to a stable and satisfying marriage."[2]

Communication is the lifeblood of marriage. Having difficulties with communication does not bode well for marital satisfaction.[3] In fact, one of the most important skills you can learn is how to talk so your mate will listen and how to listen so your mate will talk.

Maybe you think you already know how to communicate. Like most engaged couples we counsel, you are saying, "We are in love, we can talk about anything." But did you know your partner lives by different rules of communication than you do? Everyone grows up with a unique set of communication "rules," and marriage forces two people with different sets of rules to renegotiate them.

Robert and Melissa, for example, were madly in love. Before they were married they talked late into the night and spent countless hours on the phone. But they soon learned communication isn't always easy. "Just before we got married," Melissa told us, "Robert came to one of my family's get-togethers, but he hardly spoke. If somebody interrupted him in the middle of a story or a comment, Rob would just shut down. It drove me nuts."

"It took me a while to catch on," Robert told us. "In Melissa's family, interrupting is a sign of involvement. It means they are listening to you, and that was new to me. In my family everyone politely takes turns responding to the previous comment. I never understood why Melissa thought my family was so boring and stilted."

After learning some new rules for communication and adjusting some old ones, Melissa said, "It helped us both to realize there are not 'right' or 'wrong' styles of conversation; there are simply different styles."

Robert and Melissa solved a lot of potential problems early in their marriage—before they even emerged. You can, too. Next we consider how easy it is for communication to get derailed.

Workbook Exercise 15
How Well Do You Communicate?

Communication obstacles exist between every husband and wife. The workbook exercise *How Well Do You Communicate?* will help you and your partner identify potential barriers and overcome them before they overcome you.

HOW NOT TO COMMUNICATE

A cartoon depicts a grumpy husband reading the paper, his aggrieved wife standing in front of him, arms folded. He is saying, "Do we have to try to save our marriage while I'm reading the sports page?" His reaction points to one of the most common complaints of unhappy spouses: "He/she doesn't talk to me."

Whenever a marriage is disintegrating, the partners conclude, "We just can't communicate" or "We just don't talk to each other anymore." They believe the failure to talk is the cause of their problems. Actually, the nontalking is not a *lack* of communication but a *form* of communication that sends a surplus of negative messages. Silence is a powerful communicator. Laurens Van der Post's novel *The Face Beside the Fire* tells the story of a woman and the husband she had ceased to love. "Slowly she is poisoning Albert.... The poison ... is found in no chemist's book.... It is a poison brewed from all the words, the delicate, tender, burning trivialities and petty endearments she never used—but would have spoken if she'd truly loved him."[4]

Silence, however powerful, is not the cause of poor communication—the fear of pain is. It is basic to human nature to seek pleasure and avoid pain. But people actually avoid pain first and then seek pleasure. This point is crucial to understanding breakdowns in communication because most of them occur when we urgently want to avoid the emotional pain of feeling inadequate, vulnerable, fearful, and so on. Under these potentially painful circumstances communication goes awry. When we feel inadequate, we are communicating: "If you really knew what I was like, you might not like me." When we feel vulnerable: "If I told you my real feelings, you might hurt me." Fearful: "If I expressed my anger, it would destroy you" or "If I told you how I felt, you would get angry."

Noted family therapist Virginia Satir talks about four styles of miscommunication that result when we feel threatened: (1) placating, (2) blaming, (3) computing, and (4) distracting.[5] Each style is a dysfunctional response to potential pain, and each frustrates our attempts to understand what our partner wants us to hear.

PLACATING

The placater is a "yes" man or woman, ingratiating, eager to please, and apologetic. Placaters say things like "Whatever you want" or "Never mind about me, it's okay." They want to keep the peace at any price, and the price they pay is feelings of worthlessness. Because placaters have difficulty expressing anger and hold so many feelings inside, they tend toward depression and, as studies show, may be prone to illness. Placaters need to know it is okay to disagree.

BLAMING

The blamer is a fault-finder who criticizes relentlessly and speaks in generalizations: "You never do anything right." "You're just like your mother." Inside, blamers feel unworthy or unlovable, angry at the anticipation they will not get what they want. Given a problem, blamers feel the best defense is a good offense, because they are incapable of dealing with or expressing pain or fear. Blamers need to be able to speak on their own behalf without indicting others in the process.

COMPUTING

The computer is super-reasonable, stays calm and collected, never admits mistakes, and expects people to conform and perform. The computer says things like "Upset? I'm not upset. Why do you say I'm upset?" Afraid of emotion, he or she prefers facts and statistics. "I don't reveal my emotions, and I'm not interested in anyone else's." Computers need someone to ask how they feel about specific things.

DISTRACTING

The distracter resorts to irrelevancies under stress, avoiding direct eye contact and direct answers. Quick to change the subject, he or she will say, "What problem? Let's go shopping." Confronting the problem might lead to a fight, which could be dangerous. Distracters need to know that they are safe, not helpless, that problems can be solved and conflicts resolved.

The next time you find yourself communicating with your partner by placating, blaming, computing, or distracting, remember that you are probably feeling hurt or stressed out about something. Also, if your partner is resorting to one of these styles, you can ease his or her tension by being sensitive to what might really be at the root of it. The upshot is that you need to find a way to make it safe for both of you to talk. And this is done by laying down a solid foundation for effective communication.

Workbook Exercise 16
The Daily Temperature Reading

How can you say what you really mean in a way that your partner can hear it? The workbook exercise *The Daily Temperature Reading* will help you and your partner send and receive messages that will be accurately understood.

THE BEDROCK OF SUCCESSFUL COMMUNICATION

The happiest couples we know have relatively few communication impasses. They are able to talk easily about difficult subjects; they feel they understand each other; they withhold very little from each other; and they rely on their ability to resolve conflicts. Their secret is not a list of communication "rules," it is understanding this: *Good communication is built first on who you are—and only later on what you do.* Before practicing communication "techniques," these couples work on who they are as people.

You can read articles and books, attend workshops, and see counselors that will all teach you communication *skills*, but if you do not first focus on the *qualities* you possess as a partner, your efforts will be of little consequence. To enjoy rich communication and a rock-solid marriage, three personal qualities must be present: warmth, genuineness, and empathy.

WARMTH

Your partner came to you with a cluster of unacceptable qualities, some known, many still to be discovered. Yet you, as a spouse, have chosen to accept him or her anyway. You have decided to embrace your partner in spite of bad breath, blemishes, quirky behaviors, and weird inclinations. That is the stuff of personal warmth — overlooking a blemish for the sake of the beauty behind it.

The key to personal warmth is acceptance. Rather than evaluating or requiring change, you simply accept the thoughts, feelings, and actions of the person you love.

It took me a long time to give Leslie permission to be who she is. Leslie has a lighthearted gift for smelling the roses, whenever and wherever she finds them, even if it means putting off some chores. I have a gift for plowing through obstacles and getting things done quickly. Early in our marriage I thought I had a calling to convert Leslie to my work ethic. But my missionary efforts made us both miserable. Once I learned the way of warmth and embraced her way of being, we enjoyed a much more interesting and happy partnership.

Warmth is not a carte blanche approval of anything your spouse does, nor is it a kind of smothering sentimentality of contrived emotion. Warmth invites your partner to be who she is, relaxed, free, and at peace. It bolsters her confidence and keeps her from contorting her personality into what she thinks you want it to be.

Unconditional warmth also invites God's grace into the soul of your marriage. When your partner feels sure that she can never be condemned by you for who she is, that no judgment can hurt her, God's grace has seeped into the fabric of your relationship — stopping the subtle and unhealthy marital pattern of your partner continually casting about for your approval.

GENUINENESS

Your partner has a built-in radar detector for phoniness, spotting fabricated feelings and insincere intentions long before they are openly expressed. Your partner will not trust you if he or she feels you are not genuine. Without genuineness, little else in marriage matters.

How is genuineness expressed? Not in words. What you say to your partner is far less important than how you say it — with a smile, a shrug, a frown, or a glare. Consider this: Nonverbal communication accounts for 58 percent of the total message. Tone of voice makes up 35 percent of the message. The actual words you say account for only 7 percent of the total message.

Genuineness is expressed in your tone and nonverbal behavior, your eyes and your posture. And research has found that husbands and wives are very accurate interpreters of their spouse's nonverbal communication.[6] An acquaintance may not notice a subtle change in your facial expression, but your spouse will.

When we got married, I was so eager to be the perfect wife that I tried to think, feel, and do everything I thought perfect wives were supposed to. But instead of being perfect, I ended up feeling empty. I was playing a role instead of being myself. Fortunately, a skilled counselor helped me when he said, "Leslie, you are more concerned with the question 'What *should* I be feeling?' than you are with the question 'What *am* I feeling?'" He was right. I decided that what our marriage needed most was not a perfect partner, but me as a genuine person.

You can shower your partner with love, but if you're not real, the love is hollow. You can use all the communication techniques in the world, but if you aren't genuine, they won't work. Authenticity is something you *are*, not something you *do*. It comes from the heart, not the hands.

EMPATHY

The best way to avoid stepping on your mate's toes is to put yourself into his or her shoes. That's empathy—seeing the world from your partner's perspective.

Several years ago I (Les) was conducting training seminars for elementary school teachers. To help them better understand the world of a third grader, I gave them the assignment of walking through their classroom on their knees. "I always assumed students were viewing the classroom as I was," said one teacher after completing the exercise. "It looks so different from their perspective."

We make the same error in marriage when we assume our spouses know what we are experiencing. They don't. Everyone interprets life from a composite of unique insights and perceptions. Life looks different for our spouse than it does for us, yet we tend to assume that he or she sees life as we see it. Only after entering their world with both heart and head, however, can we accurately understand their perspective.

To look at life through the same lens means asking yourself two questions: (1) What does this situation, problem, or event look or feel like from my partner's perspective? and (2) How is his or her perception different from mine?

> Do not let any unwholesome talk come out of your mouths, but only what is helpful for building others up according to their needs.
>
> Ephesians 4:29

Developing empathy is perhaps the toughest task in building a strong marriage. Because most of us are wired to use either our head or heart—one more than the other—it takes a conscious effort to empathize. In our book *Trading Places*, we describe how loving with our heart alone is only sympathizing, while loving with our head alone is simply analyzing. Empathy, however, brings together both sympathetic and analytic abilities, both heart and head, to fully understand our partners. Empathy says, "If I were you, I would act as you do; I understand why you feel the way you feel."

Empathy always involves risk, so be forewarned. Accurately understanding your partner's hurts and hopes will change you—but the benefits of taking that risk far outweigh the disadvantages. Once you consciously feel his or her feelings and understand his or her perspective, you will see the world differently.

The bedrock of communication is secured in who you are as a person—in being warm, genuine, and empathetic. But while these three traits are critical for effective communication, by themselves they do not assure success. A few simple "rules" are still needed.

"RULES" FOR SUCCESSFUL COMMUNICATION

All the important communication tools can be reduced to five basic skills. If you learn them and use them, you will be able to give more love to your spouse, and your marriage will become supercharged with positive energy.

They are:

1. Make "I" statements, not "you" statements.
2. Practice reflective listening.
3. Understand and accept the differences between men and women.
4. Apologize when necessary.
5. Power down and get offline
6. Communicate through touch.

MAKE "I" STATEMENTS, NOT "YOU" STATEMENTS

When you are upset with your partner or you feel hurt by him or her, your natural tendency is to attack: "You drive me crazy! You never ask my opinion when you decide something important!"

A "you" statement like this guarantees a relational barrier. Your partner has virtually no alternative but to feel blamed, accused, and criticized. It is extremely unlikely that he or she will say, "Yes, you are right. I can be very insensitive." Rather, his or her natural reaction will be defensive: "What do you mean? If you have an opinion, just say it. I can't read your mind."

And then what typically follows is a returned "you" statement. "You are the one that's insensitive. Did you ever consider the pressure I'm under right now?"

Volleying "you" statements is a surefire way to spoil an evening. This scene would be completely different had "I" statements been used to report how you felt or how you experienced the situation: "I feel hurt and neglected when you don't ask my opinion."

Do you sense the difference? "I" statements dispense information to be understood rather than accusations to be defended. "I" statements are much more likely to elicit concern and caring from your partner: "I'm sorry, honey. I had no idea you were feeling that way." "I" statements do not cause defensiveness because they say nothing about how bad your spouse is.

There is no benefit to your spouse's feeling attacked. Instead of saying, "You are so careless. How could you forget that we were going out tonight?" it would be better to say, "I feel hurt and a little scared when you forget things we plan together." This allows you to express your feeling of being neglected, but you're saying it without accusing your partner of intentionally hurting you.

In place of "You try to make me feel stupid by always correcting what I say," say something like "I feel very put down when you correct little things I say." Begin your sentences with "I" rather than "you," and you will save your marriage much misery.

Communication is not what you say, but what your partner understands by what you say. When you make "you" statements, all your partner hears is blame and criticism. "I" statements are much more effective, because they allow your message to be correctly heard and understood.

PRACTICE REFLECTIVE LISTENING

A sage once said that the Lord gave us two ears and one mouth, and that ration ought to tell us something. Good point. We often think about learning "good communication skills" as learning to express ourselves more clearly, getting our message across. In fact, however, 98 percent of good communication is listening.

If you can hear, you can listen—right? Wrong. Hearing is passive. Listening is *actively* interacting with a message by reflecting it back to the sender. Effective listening is a simple habit to develop, but it can be difficult to learn because in situations where it is most important, we are usually more focused on what we are going to say next than we are on listening to the message being sent.

Consider this typical husband/wife interaction:

Wife: *(holding up a navy-blue dress with a broad white collar)* Look at this! I just got this dress cleaned, and there's a gray stain all over the collar! I can't believe it. What am I going to do now? I was going to wear this dress tonight!

Husband: Oh, honey, I don't think anyone would even notice it. Besides, you could wear your yellow dress. It looks great.

The husband in this scenario was trying to be helpful, but he didn't listen. He was more concerned with solving the problem than with understanding his wife's emotions. He could have made any number of remarks that would have made his wife feel heard and understood, such as "I'm so sorry, I'd be furious too" or "I can't imagine how disappointed you are."

> Be quick to listen and slow to speak.
>
> James 1:19

The point of reflective listening is to let your partner know that you have heard what they said and that you understand their message. By the way, reflective listening is a wonderful way to defuse a potential conflict. If your partner starts hurling "you" statements such as "You are always late," don't say, "I am not." Instead genuinely express your understanding of his or her feelings by saying, "I know it upsets you when I'm late. It's got to be exasperating. I'll work on being on time in the future." Listen for the message underlying the actual words. "You are always late" means "I'm upset."

Many of the couples we teach reflective listening to complain that it feels awkward and sounds phony or even patronizing. That's why we lay a foundation with being warm, genuine, and empathetic. When reflective listening is grounded in these traits, it is never a robotic function; it comes from the heart. If you are listening deeply, and if you truly care, then what you reflect back to your partner will not be mechanical. Like any new skill, reflective listening may feel awkward at first, but when you begin to experience the difference it makes in your marriage, the awkward feeling will abate quickly.

Remember, however, that true empathy in listening involves *change*. Unfortunately, some people may learn to listen well, but they fail to heed what they hear. If your partner is asking for a change in your behavior, seriously consider the request and then, if it seems reasonable, act on it. Just as words without deeds are dead, so is listening without action.

One more thing on listening. If you are at a loss and can't seem to reflect your partner's message, do two things: (1) make sure you really want to accurately understand their message, and (2) say something like "Tell me more about it" or "Help me understand what you mean." This safety-net technique works wonders.

Renowned Swiss counselor Dr. Paul Tournier has said, "It is impossible to overemphasize the immense need we have to be really listened to, to be taken seriously, to be understood.... No one can develop freely in this world and find a full life without feeling understood by at least one person."[7] When you offer your spouse the gift of listening, you are embodying what marriage was meant to be.

Workbook Exercise 17
I Can Hear Clearly Now

Learning to reflect your partner's emotional message is critical to good communication. The workbook exercise *I Can Hear Clearly Now* will help you and your partner genuinely convey your understanding of each other by reflecting what you hear.

UNDERSTAND AND ACCEPT THE DIFFERENCES BETWEEN MEN AND WOMEN

When Professor Henry Higgins cries out in *My Fair Lady*, "Why can't a woman be more like a man?" we all know he's not talking about anatomy. He's in love with Eliza, but he can't really understand her. An expert in languages, he has taught Eliza how to speak English his upper-class way, but he can't really communicate with her.

Henry Higgins is not alone. Almost every man and every woman has at some point despaired of ever getting through to the opposite sex. Men and women are very different. While our roles can be changed, our psyches cannot. And even though the other sex's behavior is different from ours, it is not wrong. If we judge it as "bad," we are simply being myopic and old-fashioned. We must accept our differences, quit railing against them, change our expectations, and accept each other. Accepting each other's differences is a vital key to effective communication.

> Often the difference between a successful marriage and a mediocre one consists of leaving about three or four things a day unsaid.
>
> Harlan Miller

Communication can either span or widen the gender gap. In conversation, men and women appear to be doing the same thing—they open their mouths and produce noise. However, they actually use conversation for quite different purposes. Women use conversation primarily to form and solidify connections with other people. Men, on the other hand, tend to use words to navigate their way within the hierarchy by communicating their knowledge and skill and imparting information.

Women excel at what linguistics expert Deborah Tannen calls "rapport-talk." Men feel most comfortable with "report-talk."[8] Even though women may have more confidence in verbal ability (aptitude tests prove their superior skill), they are less likely to use that ability in a public context. Men feel comfortable giving reports to groups or interrupting a speaker with an objection—these are skills learned in the male hierarchy. Many women might perceive the same behavior as putting themselves on display. For example, at a party the men tell stories, share their expertise, and tell jokes, while the women usually converse in smaller groups about more personal subjects. They are busy connecting, while the men are positioning themselves.

How does this relate to communicating within your marriage? It comes down to this: Conversationally speaking, women share feelings, and men solve problems. If you do not comprehend this stylistic difference, your conversations can be terribly frustrating. For example:

Wife: You won't believe the amount of work my boss is giving me. Listen to this . . .
Husband: Honey, I keep telling you to talk to him about that.

These kinds of interactions send too many couples to counselors because they don't understand that women share feelings and men solve problems. Once this distinction is made, a simple solution can be applied that works instantly and with very little practice: Simply label the type of conversation you want to have and ask your partner to join you. Just because men have a tendency to solve problems and women have a tendency to share feelings doesn't mean that each isn't capable of the other mode. Here's how the above conversation could have proceeded:

She: You won't believe the amount of work my boss is giving me. Listen to this. . .
He: Honey, I keep telling you to talk to him about that.
She: I know, but I'd like to have a feelings conversation right now, okay? I just need to get this out.
He: Okay, tell me about it.

At that point, she can relate the incident and he can actively listen to her feelings, reflecting them back to her from time to time. When you realize the two of you are in different modes, labeling a conversation "feeling-talk" or "problem-talk" works magic, honoring both styles in your marriage and validating your partner's communication gifts.

We'll have much more to say about gender differences in the next chapter.

> Words! Words! I'm so sick of words! I get words all day through. Is that all you blighters can do? Don't talk of stars burning above. If you're in love, show me!
>
> Eliza in *My Fair Lady*

APOLOGIZE WHEN NECESSARY

A graceful apology is a curtsy to civility, a gesture that helps crowded citizens put up with each other, a modest bow to keep hassles within tolerable bounds. But within a marriage, an apology to your partner that is sincerely meant is much more than a civility—it can be a powerful tool for resolving issues and strengthening your relationship.

Sometimes apologizing is perfectly straightforward. When one partner blows it, and the offense is minor (maybe he forgot to put gas in the car), a graceful apology is all it takes for the incident to be dropped. At other times an apology can be surprisingly complicated.

Like lots of couples, one husband and wife we worked with would regularly short-circuit their arguments with hasty apologies. "I said I was sorry for what I did," one of them would say. "Now why can't you forget about it and move on?"

This form of apology is really a tool of manipulation, a way of getting off the hook and avoiding the real issue. What's worse, a premature apology blocks real change. One husband snapped at his wife at a dinner party. Later he said, "I'm sorry, but look, you have to understand that I've been under a lot of stress lately." The husband was avoiding responsibility for his insensitive behavior. What his wife needed to hear was "I'm sorry. It isn't right to lash out at you when I'm stressed." This would have told the wife that her husband understood he had hurt her and would try not to do it again.

True apologies in marriage can happen only when partners come to understand accountability. This is another way of saying that each of you must take responsibility for your own behavior, acknowledge your partner's point of view, and at times own up to things about yourself you don't like. Finally, it may mean making changes. "I had to swallow my pride and admit to something unlikable about myself," one husband told us. "But once I did, I started changing."

All couples need a healing mechanism, a way to turn a new page in marriage, and knowing how and when to say you're sorry can make a big difference. Ask yourself when and how you apologize. Does one of you apologize more than the other? Do you use apologies to short-circuit or whitewash issues?

An apology may not be a literal "I'm sorry"; it may be giving gifts, sharing an evening out, or simply taking a quiet walk together. The point is that a sincere apology, whatever its form, leaves the couple with a renewed closeness and a relieved feeling that all is well.

POWER DOWN AND GET OFFLINE

Ready for some startling news? Couples who engage in discussions with their phones nearby—even if neither is actually using it—report lower relationship quality and feel their partner is less empathic to their concerns.[9] Ouch! This is hard to hear but research shows that our laptops, tablets, phones, and even smart watches (and the social media platforms they support) have the potential to come between couples. So much so that comedian Will Ferrell says, "Before you get married ask yourself: is this the person you want to watch stare at their phone the rest of your life?"

Consider this:

- 34 percent of couples admit to answering their phone during "intimate" moments.
- 20 percent of people would rather go shoeless for a week than take a break from their phones.
- 65 percent of people sleep next to their phones.

Is it any wonder technology is keeping us from connecting? Experts point to the fact that our gadgets provide a sense of instant gratification that stimulates our brain's reward centers. We literally become addicted. Checking our phone becomes a compulsion.

So what can you do? For starters, phones are best kept out of sight and out of mind when you're having an important conversation, when you're sharing a meal, and when it's your date night. In other words, bite the bullet and turn it off. We know this is tough, but if you make a habit of it you'll reap incredible conversations.

Experts also recommend keeping and charging your gadgets in a room other than your bedroom so they don't crimp intimacy. The bottom line is that interacting without a phone nearby helps foster closeness, connectedness, interpersonal trust, and perceptions of empathy—the building blocks of good conversations.[10]

Speaking from personal experience, I (Les) after years of getting it wrong, have made a habit of docking my phone in my home office as opposed to bringing it to dinner and to bed. That simple shift changed everything.

COMMUNICATE THROUGH TOUCH

In the last twenty years we have recognized how much infants need to be held and touched. We now know that they cannot grow—they literally fail to thrive—unless they experience physical and emotional closeness with another human being. What we often don't realize is that when we grow up the need for physical connection does not go away, and when we meet this need for our spouses we can increase the health of our marriages.

Physical contact is a powerful means of communicating and a gentle and supportive way to nourish the spirit and convey positive emotions. In her book *Anatomy of Love*, anthropologist Helen Fisher describes why touching is so powerful. "Human skin is like a field of grass, each blade a nerve ending so sensitive that the slightest graze can etch into the human brain a memory of the moment."[11]

Technically speaking, human skin is dotted with millions of nerve endings, called "touch receptors," and when you are touched, these receptors send messages to the brain. The brain, in turn, secretes chemicals appropriate to the situation.

Imagine for a moment that you come home from a tough day, feeling tense, tired, and irritable—but then your partner wraps you in his or her arms and gives you a loving squeeze. That hug causes a rise in hemoglobin, a substance in the red blood cells that transports energizing oxygen throughout your body. Incredibly, that gentle hug or even a soft caress can cause a speeding heart to quiet, soaring blood pressure to drop, and severe pain to ease.

You are probably saying, "Touching is one skill we don't have to learn." You are probably right. Communicating through touch isn't an issue with most couples who are about to wed. Typically, they hug and kiss and hold hands whenever they're together. Typically, too, they assume that's how it will always be. And, yes, in some marriages the two partners do remain huggers and handholders throughout their lives. But in many other marriages that early touching wanes. Especially after kids come along and the pace of life quickens, touching is often reserved for sex. Purely affectionate touching, except for little pats and quick kisses, may get left behind.

To help sustain your high-touch relationship, talk about how touch was used in the homes you grew up in. Was your family "high contact" or "low contact"? All the research shows a direct relationship between how you experience touching as an adult and how often and in what ways you were touched as a child. You could discuss how

131

to become more touch-oriented, even if you grew up in a family that shunned physical contact.

You might also explore each other's comfort zones. Both of you probably prefer different amounts and kinds of touching. For one of you a soft touch on the hand may mean as much as a lingering embrace to another. And studies show that some men, when they feel insecure, interpret touching as a type of put-down rather than as a source of comfort.

Given its potent impact on our lives, it's no wonder that touch is known as the "mother of the senses." There is simply no better way to communicate the idea that "You are not alone," "You're important," "I'm sorry," or "I love you." So the next time you're at a loss for words, remember, touching may be the best way of speaking to your partner.

FOR REFLECTION

1. What are your personal strengths and challenges when it comes to effective communication? And what have you learned from your first marriage about how you communicate?

2. Can you recall a conversation you had with your partner that led to confusion and pain? Looking back on it, what do you think went wrong? In other words, what will you do differently the next time a similar situation arises?

3. It is a common misconception to believe that a lack of talking is what leads to a breakdown in communication. Why isn't this so? What is the fundamental cause of dysfunctional communication?

4. Why is it important to focus first on who you are as a person before practicing communication techniques?

5. Empathy involves both thinking and feeling. What does this mean? How do you know you are empathizing with another person?

6. How does turning "you" statements into "I" statements make a difference in communication?

7. Reflecting your partner's messages lets him know you understand what he is saying. Before practicing this technique, what must a person be sure to do so that it is not simply a robotic function?

8. Studies say that men "report-talk" and women "rapport-talk." Do you find this to be true? What examples from your own experience can you think of?

9. Do you agree that physical touch plays an important part in effective communication with your partner? Why or why not?

HAVE YOU BRIDGED THE GENDER GAP?

I am a man and you are a woman. I can't think of a better arrangement.

GROUCHO MARX

You aren't really going to pack all those clothes, are you? This is a three-night trip, not three weeks. Besides, who cares how you look when you're camping?" I (Les) instantly regretted the words as they came out of my mouth. It was nearly midnight, and we were both a little testy. Early the next morning we were leaving for a weekend trip to a rustic camp near Santa Barbara.

"You take what you want, and I take what I want," Leslie replied. "Just because you are content to wear the same pair of jeans for three days, don't expect me to do the same. Anyway, what about your laptop computer? Last time we flew back East we ended up lugging that thing all over the place, and you never even turned it on. So who is being frivolous about what he packs?"

"I like knowing my computer is there if I want to use it."

"Well, I like having these clothes if I want to wear them," Leslie replied.

"You're right, you're right," I confessed. "What seems essential to me can be incidental to you and vice versa. At times we are just so different."

Different indeed. In recent years researchers have discovered that women and men have different biological, psychological, and professional realities. Biologically, women have larger connections between the two hemispheres of their brains and a tendency toward superior verbal ability. Men's greater brain hemisphere separation may contribute a slight tendency toward abstract reasoning and a superior capacity to mentally rotate objects in space.[1] Psychologically, women frequently find their sense of identity through relationships with others; men tend to find their sense of self through being separate.

Professionally, men are often more focused on long-range goals; women are frequently more attentive to the process by which those goals are achieved.

> There are four things that are too mysterious for me to understand: an eagle flying in the sky, a snake moving on a rock, a ship finding its way over the sea, and a man and woman falling in love.
>
> Proverbs 30:18 – 19

The contrasts between women and men are sometimes so striking one wonders how the attraction between them can be so strong. It's a puzzle humans have tried to solve for centuries. An ancient Greek myth tells of the earth being populated by beings who were half-man, half-woman. They were each complete in themselves and deemed themselves perfect. In their pride they rebelled against the gods, whereupon the irate Zeus split each of them in half, scattering the halves over the earth. Ever since, the myth has it, each half has been searching for its other half.

There must be some subtle fragment of truth in this mythical explanation. The story of Creation underscores the fundamental fact of our need of each other because of our differences. Adam, living in the only Paradise that has ever existed on this earth, felt no pain and shed no tears. And yet even in Paradise loneliness flourished, so much so that God determined it was not "good" for man to be alone—something was missing. God responded by creating Eve.

There is an inherent completeness when a man and woman marry. Our partner makes up for what we lack. When we are discouraged, they are hopeful. When we are stingy, they are generous. When we are weak, they are strong. Because we are male and female joined together, there is wholeness. But our differences, if not understood and accepted, become a source of confusion rather than completeness.

Too often in marriage the fundamental differences between women and men are overlooked when we mistakenly assume that our partners are just like us—"what is good for me is good for you." We evaluate their behavior according to our feminine or masculine standards, never considering the vast differences between the sexes.

For many years, gender differences were not clearly defined. But we now recognize, more precisely than ever before, the gap between men and women. And to ignore this gap is to risk putting your marriage on the brink of disaster.

SYMBIS Report Page 13
Do You Know What You Need
from Each Other?

You already know that men and women are different. But do you know how your differences drive your deepest needs — especially when combined with your unique personalities?

If you're using the SYMBIS Assessment, you'll discover your personalized list of deep needs and how your partner can fulfill them. This information can save both of you years of missing the mark when it comes to loving at the deepest level. Your personalized report will show each of you how to best meet the other's needs.

The purpose of this chapter is to help you recognize that your partner, by virtue of being the opposite sex, thinks, feels, and behaves differently than you do. Those differences, if heeded and accounted for, can become the source of greater intimacy in your marriage.[2] We begin by underscoring the fact that men and women are different and by looking at exactly how men and women are different. Then we show you, as male and female, how to bridge the gender gap and live successfully with the opposite sex—living in "oneness" as woman and man.

ARE WE *THAT* DIFFERENT?

The feminist revolution of the 1970s made talk of inborn differences in the behavior of men and women distinctly unfashionable, even taboo. Once sexism was abolished, so the argument ran, the world would become a perfectly equitable, androgynous place, aside from a few anatomical details. Male-female differences were not inborn, they argued, but simply learned, and thus could be unlearned.

> In our civilization men are afraid they will not be man enough, and women are afraid that they might be considered only women.
>
> Theodore Reik

But rather than disappear, the evidence for innate gender differences began to mount. Scientists, for example, uncovered neurological differences between the sexes both in the brain's structure and in its functioning, forcing every objective thinker to conclude that nature is at least as important as nurture after all. Even Betty Friedan, catalyst for much of the feminist movement, was later compelled to chide her feminist sisters: "The time has come to acknowledge that women are different than men. There has to be equality that takes into account that women are the ones who have the babies."[3] *Vive la difference.*

While science has shown that men and women are in fact wired differently—that gender differences have as much to do with the biology of the brain as with the way we were raised—we have difficulty accepting, let alone appreciating, our differences. And that's where a great deal of trouble in marriage begins.

Whenever we conduct a marriage retreat we eventually divide the group in half—wives in one circle, husbands in another—for a brief exercise. We then ask a question that always generates a lively discussion among the same-sex groups: What do men need to know about women, and what do women need to know about men? The responses are predictable:

Men say ...	Women say ...
• women are too emotional	• men aren't sensitive enough
• women don't feel as much pressure to provide the family's income	• men don't do their fair share of the housework
• women frequently deny their real power	• men are afraid to be vulnerable or out of control
• women talk too much	• men don't listen

The point of our exercise is not to gripe about the opposite sex but to help couples see, first of all, that there are predictable differences between the sexes, and second, to realize that the differences they thought were personal, strictly between them and their spouse, are often shared by most other couples. "I thought we were marriage mutants before this exercise," one couple told us. "Just realizing how universal our differences are lets us know we are normal and can make it work."

Making marriage work, however, does not depend solely on recognizing our differences. It's a matter of *appreciating* those differences, too. We have seen some couples identify their differences and then try to eliminate them. Wayne, for example, decided Teri's more expressive emotion needed to be curbed. "There is no need to spend your energy on getting so emotional," he would say. Wanting to be a team player, Teri tried desperately to stifle her natural expressions of emotion and be more like Wayne. Both were sincere in their efforts to bridge the gender gap, but they were doomed from the beginning. Gender differences are not eased by creating symmetry—by having men and women thinking, feeling, and doing everything alike. The fact is that men and women *are* different. And couples who openly acknowledge their differences and appreciate them improve their chances of avoiding strife. Plus, they increase their level of intimacy by delighting in their differences. The key, of course, is knowing exactly what those differences are.

Workbook Exercise 18
Couple's Inventory

As you bridge the gender gap, each of you will operate with differing assumptions. The workbook exercise *Couple's Inventory* will help you and your partner look at how your gender-role assumptions influence decision making and intimacy in your relationship.

HOW ARE WE DIFFERENT?

You'll always find exceptions to the rule, but research and experience consistently point to a fundamental and powerful distinction between the sexes: *Men focus on achievement, women focus on relationships*. It sounds overly simplistic, and it probably is.[4] But remembering this general rule can save every couple wear and tear on their marriage and strengthen their bond.

Leslie and I, like other couples, learned this essential difference between the sexes soon after we married.

LESLIE'S PERSPECTIVE

During our fourth or fifth month of marriage, I remember wondering why Les wasn't as romantic as he used to be. Before we got married he planned exciting evenings, kissed me at red traffic lights, saved ticket stubs from our dates, bought me flowers, and even wrote tender love poems. But after we got married, his romantic side waned. It wasn't that he stopped his romantic ways altogether, but something was distinctly different. *Why?* I wondered to myself. *Am I doing something wrong? Is he having doubts about our marriage?* Not until I discovered the fundamental difference between men and women could I accurately answer these questions.

Les, like the majority of men, is pragmatic. He focuses upon a future goal and needs to believe in the practical value of that goal. He justifies a present activity by what it will accomplish in the future. He asks, "What good can this produce?" He likes words like *progress* and *useful*. He can be very patient doing romantic little things, so long as they ultimately prove productive.

I, on the other hand, am like the majority of women. I focus on feelings and activities of the present—for their own sake. I don't need a goal; it is enough to simply enjoy the moment. I ask, "What is going on and how can I know and feel it?" I don't need to be productive or see the utility of something. In fact, achievement seems deadly cold and distracting. I like words like *connected* and *relational*. I can be very patient doing romantic little things simply because the doing has its own value.

Of course, Les has a different perspective.

LES'S PERSPECTIVE

Before our wedding Leslie was happy-go-lucky and eager to please. She felt good about our relationship and optimistic about the future. But soon after we married, Leslie began to change, or so it seemed to me. She became overly concerned about our relationship

141

and talked about ways to improve it. If I didn't join in, she'd feel hurt and rejected. *Why has she so suddenly become emotional?* I remember thinking. *Why does she cry so easily now?* Before we got married she never seemed so impractical; now, at times, she seemed irrational to me. *How could flowers be so important when we can hardly make ends meet?* I'd wonder. Her desire to talk about our relationship made me feel I was a failure as a husband. *Doesn't she appreciate all I do for her?* I'd think.

I, like most men, didn't feel the need to have lengthy discussions about our relationship. I was content to know that Leslie loved me, I loved her, and we were on our way to a happy life together. What's to discuss? Getting all worked up over this or that detail was a waste of energy, from my perspective.

THE BOTTOM LINE

Recognizing how fundamentally different men and women are allowed me (Leslie) to see that Les courted me to get married. It's that simple. Once we married, his purpose of courtship was accomplished, and he was ready to move on to other productive activities. It turned out that his "sweet nothings" were not "nothings" after all, but whisperings calculated to persuade me to the altar. It sounds deceptive, but it's not. In fact, Les presumed that I was just like him and that we would both continue romancing each other only so long as it had a practical consequence; after that he expected us both to move on to the real business of living.

> Your willingness to accept the differences between you will allow you to complement one another in ways that make life better for each of you.
>
> C. W. Neal

I (Les) eventually realized that neither of us really changed after marriage. But our circumstances did. The goal that made me especially romantic was met, and the romance for romance's sake that Leslie valued was no longer a shared priority in the relationship. Because my energies were shifting to more practical matters of building a stable home with a secure future, it was hard for me to realize that Leslie did not see it exactly like me. She wanted to court and kiss for kissing's sake. And once married, she expected the same style of romance to continue forever.

Our differences are not unique. They are universal: Men are motivated by achievement, women by relationships.[5] So when gender differences emerge in your marriage, don't judge your spouse as evil. He or she did not deceive you; it simply took marriage to reveal your differences.

The differences you bring together as woman and man are good and can be celebrated. As one body must have both a calculating head and a feeling heart, so one marriage is blessed with both gifts. We are fearfully and wonderfully made.

So how do you celebrate male-female differences? By meeting the unique needs that are part of your spouse's gender. Typically, men try to meet the needs that men value, and women try to meet the needs that women value. The trouble is, your husband's needs are not the same as your needs, and you cannot meet his needs by doing what you would do for another woman. In the same way, a wife's needs are different from her husband's, and he cannot meet her needs by doing what comes naturally to a man. In essence, both husbands and wives must "stretch" beyond themselves, taking into consideration what their spouses need, then providing it.

In the following two sections we pinpoint a few specific needs that you may not realize your partner has. By meeting these needs for your partner, you will bridge the gender gap in your marriage and reap countless rewards.

Workbook Exercise 19
Your Top Ten Needs

Men and women have different needs in marriage. Without knowing what your partner's greatest needs are, you will fail miserably in trying to meet them. The workbook exercise *Your Top Ten Needs* will help you and your partner identify how your personal needs differ.

WHAT EVERY HUSBAND SHOULD KNOW ABOUT HIS WIFE

Sigmund Freud, the father of psychoanalysis, said, "Despite my thirty years of research into the feminine soul, I have not yet been able to answer the great question: What does a woman want?"

Well, Freud may not have been able to identify the deepest needs of women, but modern research has.[6] A wife's most basic needs in marriage are: (1) to be cherished, (2) to be known, and (3) to be respected.

SHE NEEDS TO BE CHERISHED

"I can't understand it, Doc." Doug was talking before he even sat down in my counseling office. "Lisa has everything she could possibly need. She doesn't have to work, she buys lots of clothes, we live in a great place, we take wonderful vacations, I'm faithful—but she's miserable." Doug shook his head and said, "I just don't get it."

We talked a bit more about his seven-year marriage and how he tried to express his love for Lisa. "I'm not the talkative type, Doc," he said. "I show my love by providing the very best I can for her." This poor husband didn't realize that his love-starved wife would have traded all the clothes and vacations in the world for a little tenderness from him.

Without meaning to, a husband can completely miss one of his wife's most important needs: to be cherished. This need is too often overlooked by husbands because we don't feel the need for it as deeply as women do. But that doesn't discount its validity. Your wife needs to be cherished. She needs to know she is number one in your life. If it came down to an evening with your buddies or a night with your wife, she needs to know you would choose her—not because you have to, but because you want to.

I once asked my pastor, Tharon Daniels, how he cherished his wife, Barbara. "I made a decision some years ago to give up golf. It sounds silly," he said, "but golf was eating up my entire day off. Golf was taking valuable time away from being with Barbara, and she's more important to me than golf." He went on to tell me that his decision was not for everyone, but it was his attempt to cherish his wife. And it worked.

What can you do to cherish your wife? Consider how often you say, "I love you." Some men don't feel the need to say it with words, but every wife has an insatiable need to hear it. Your wife also needs evidence that you are thinking about her during your day. A small gift or a quick phone call to say, "You are on my mind," can mean the world to her.

I was recently reminded of how much it means to Leslie when I send her a card or note. Sitting down at her desk at work to use her phone, I noticed a handmade card on her bulletin board that I had given her—more than five years ago.

As a man, you probably have no idea of the effect you can have on your wife by being gentle and tender, making her feel cared for. Mike, however, learned the incredible results of meeting his wife's need to be cherished. He was running late for work when Brenda said she was going to have an extremely pressure-filled day. He was almost out the door when he remembered my talking at a recent conference about a wife's need to be cherished. Mike set down his briefcase and poured a cup of coffee for Brenda. "What are you doing?" Brenda asked. "You are going to be late for work." The thought shot through his head, *She's right!* But Mike then said something that couldn't have done more to meet his wife's need to feel loved. "You are way more important than work." As the two of them talked for a moment, Mike squeezed Brenda's hand and said, "I'll be thinking about you today." Brenda was overwhelmed with love for her husband. And Mike was so amazed by her sincere gratitude that he called my office that morning to thank me.

Does cherishing your wife mean sacrificing golf games, success at work, or nights out with the boys? Believe it or not, the answer is no. When your wife is satisfied in knowing that she takes first place in your life, when she knows she is the most important thing in the world to you, she will encourage you to do the things you enjoy. It is part of the mystery of marriage: When a woman is truly, genuinely cherished, she feels free to encourage her husband's independence.

Before Doug learned to cherish Lisa, she would complain about his fishing trips. In fact, Lisa wanted a separation because "standing by a lake was more important to Doug than I was." But once Doug genuinely made Lisa number one, once he began to express true tenderness, Lisa pleasantly shocked him. "I'll cover for you at the meeting next Thursday so you can get an early start on your fishing trip if you want." Lisa made this offer because she now felt secure in her position of importance.

"To love and to cherish" is more than a phrase from your wedding vows. It is one of the most important needs your wife will ever have. By meeting it, you are sure to build a partnership that brings you both pleasure.

SHE NEEDS TO BE KNOWN

"You're not listening to me!" Leslie's statement jolted me from a near nap as I was half-hearing her talk to me from the kitchen. She stuck her head around the corner to see me stretched out on a recliner. "I have been pouring my heart out to you for the last fifteen minutes, and all you have done is sit there and give me advice."

Yes, I thought. *What's wrong with that?*

"I don't need advice," she continued. "I need to be understood!"

I did understand her. I heard every word about her tough day at work, and I even offered a few suggestions to help her make it better. But that's not what she needed. For a woman, being understood means having her feelings validated and accepted.

That's not as easy as it sounds. I'm a psychologist. I often spend my day doing just that with my clients. I know how to empathize with a person's pain, to feel his feelings and convey understanding. But when it comes to my marriage, something makes me want to solve Leslie's problems instead of understand them. She will tell me about something and I will passively listen until I have heard enough, and then, as if to say I'm ready to move on to other things, I will offer advice. I'll lecture instead of listen. To this day, it often takes every ounce of self-control I can muster to bite my tongue and actively listen.

At least I'm not alone. Consider this fact: Men say three times as many words in public as they do in private, while women say three times as many words in private as they do in public.[7] Women like to match experiences, to draw one another out, to volley in conversations. But when it comes to talking to their husbands, many women feel like the wife who told me, "Talking to my husband is like playing tennis with no one in the other court."

To meet your wife's important need to be known, you need to actively listen to her, reflecting back to her what she is saying and feeling, and genuinely wanting to understand her. This point cannot be overemphasized: *Women need to have their feelings validated and accepted.* They need to have you see and experience the world the way they do, instead of explaining to them why they shouldn't see it that way.

Men have a tough time realizing that offering a listening ear is all a woman needs at times — or a comforting hug, a loving statement like "You are hurting, aren't you?" or "You are under a lot of pressure, aren't you?" Listening to your wife talk without offering quick solutions is the only way to meet her need to be known.

SHE NEEDS TO BE RESPECTED

Men are usually quite unaware of how much women need to be respected. Why? Because when men are not respected they react very differently. A man who does not feel respected, for example, is apt to become self-righteous and indignant. He feels even more worthy of respect when others don't respect him. He may even give less until he gets what he feels he deserves. Women operate differently — when they are not respected they feel insecure and lose their sense of self. That is why it is so vital for you to take special care of your partner's need for respect.

There are a number of ways to show respect to your wife. To begin with, do not try to change or manipulate her, but rather, honor her needs, wishes, values, and rights. I know a woman who, because of her upbringing, valued the tradition of having her door opened for her by her husband. She knew the custom was kind of old-fashioned, but it meant a lot to her, and she asked her husband to do it.

Her husband never took her request seriously. "You're kidding, right?" he'd say. "Nobody does that anymore. That's why we've got power locks on the car." By laughing off his wife's request, this husband weakened his opportunity to meet one of his wife's deepest needs — to be respected.

What Women Want

To be loved, to be listened to, to be desired, to be respected, to be needed, to be trusted, and sometimes, just to be held.

What Men Want

Tickets for the World Series.

Dave Barry

Respecting your wife also means including her in decisions. I am always amazed when I find a husband who wields all the power in a marriage and makes all the decisions, regardless of what his wife thinks. I have known men who will make decisions about relocating to a new job in another part of the country without even consulting their wives. I don't know of a quicker way to tear down a woman's sense of self and ruin the possibility of a happy marriage. Build your wife's self-esteem and sense of security by asking for her input whenever you can, even on the small things. When you make a decision that might affect her, say, "I'm thinking about ... What do you think of that?" or "I'm thinking we should ... What would you like?"

Respecting your wife means supporting her in fulfilling her dreams and aspirations. I have a friend, Rich Jones, who is a businessman in Chicago. Some years ago his wife, Laura, set her sights on a career as a news reporter. After studying at Northwestern University, Laura landed her first reporting job at a small newspaper in the suburb where they lived. A couple of years later, Laura was offered an assignment as a television reporter in another state. At that point, Rich knew he was at a crossroads. He had promised to respect Laura's dream, but he never imagined it would mean moving! Well, Rich could have complained about Laura's aspirations. After all, he had a professional life too. But Rich stuck by his word and continued to respect his wife's dream, and she did the same for him. Today they are happily married back in Chicago, where Laura anchors for one of the networks.

Respect says, "I support you, you are valuable to me, and you don't have to be any different from who you are." In return for this respect a woman will be able to relax. She will not have a compulsive need to prove herself as an equal, but will automatically feel and be equal. What a wonderful way to live with a woman.

WHAT EVERY WIFE SHOULD KNOW ABOUT HER HUSBAND

No one plays as significant a role in meeting a man's unique needs as his wife. Researchers have identified his needs, but only his wife can truly satisfy them. Some of your husband's most basic needs in marriage are: (1) to be admired, (2) to have autonomy, and (3) to enjoy shared activity.

149

HE NEEDS TO BE ADMIRED

"Oh, Scott, these look great. You did a wonderful job." Kari's eyes lit up with excitement as she surveyed the planter boxes her husband had just made for their deck. "You really have talent."

"I enjoyed making them," Scott said, "but it's not that big a deal."

"You underestimate yourself, honey. You're good."

Scott didn't show it, but he was relishing his wife's praise. It felt great. No one could make him feel as admired and appreciated as Kari. And Kari knew it. She had tapped into this primarily male need and gladly filled it every opportunity she could. Kari's admiration was genuine, never insincere or overdone. She was Scott's biggest fan, and their marriage benefited in untold ways from her vocal admiration.

Being appreciated is a man's primary need. He measures his worth through his achievements, big and small, and needs them to be recognized. A woman's need for admiration and appreciation, while certainly important, is rarely as strong. When a woman seeks appreciation she is more accurately wanting to be understood, to be validated. You see, there is a significant difference between men and women when it comes to being admired. Men derive their worth more from what they *do*, while women derive their worth more from who they *are*.

Look at it this way. When women do not receive admiration from their spouse, they tend to be more motivated than ever to earn it. But when a man does not receive admiration from his spouse, he begins to lose motivation to try. Without a feeling of being admired, a man's energy is drained. He soon feels inadequate and incapable of giving support. Without being admired, men lose their will to give.

You have no idea how damaging a critical statement is to your man's personal power. He responds to not being admired the same way you do when he invalidates your feelings. It is demoralizing.

I counseled a woman who became confused when, after criticizing her husband, he did not try harder to earn appreciation from her. She mistakenly assumed that she could manipulate him to give more by withdrawing her appreciation. But that never works with a man. Admiration is the fuel a man needs to get going. It gives him power.

Now, before you begin heaping words of praise on your spouse, I need to give you a word of caution. Never fake your admiration. By simply saying flattering words to your husband, you can do more harm than good. To have any value, praise must genuinely reflect your feelings.[8]

HE NEEDS TO HAVE AUTONOMY

During our first year of marriage, I remember bursting into Les's study to let him know I was home. He was beginning a grueling doctoral program, and I had just begun a new job. "How are you doing?" I asked as I slipped behind his desk and wrapped my arms around his neck.

He sat almost motionless, taking notes on a yellow pad. So I tried again. "Did you have a good day?"

This time I heard a slight sound. "Mm-hmm," he murmured.

"You wouldn't believe all the stuff that happened to me today—" I started to say.

Les interrupted, "Give me just a minute here, okay?"

I walked out of the room feeling terribly dejected. *Why doesn't he welcome my caring for him?* I thought. *I would stop anything I was doing if he greeted me that way.*

Only later in our marriage did I realize what was actually going on. Men and women cope differently with stress. According to John Gray, author of *Men Are from Mars, Women Are from Venus*, men, when faced with stress, "become increasingly focused and withdrawn while women become increasingly overwhelmed and emotionally involved. At these times a man's needs for feeling good are different from a woman's. He feels better by solving problems while she feels better by talking about problems."[9]

Once I understood this distinction, I was able to meet one of Les's primary needs—to be autonomous. It is a universal male need.

Whenever a man is under stress (an important deadline is approaching, he is under pressure at work, etc.), he requires a little space. At such times he becomes absentminded, unresponsive, absorbed, and preoccupied. Unlike women, men typically don't want to talk about the situation, they don't want to be held or comforted—not until they have had time to themselves.

I have learned from experience that if I try too early to disengage Les from his problem, I get only a small part of his attention while he continues to mull over whatever is really on his mind. It is as if he is temporarily incapable of giving me the attention I want until he has a moment to adjust his agenda. I now know enough to say, "Is this a good time to interrupt?" and he can say, "I need another five minutes" or "I'd really like to unwind by watching the news first."

You see, part of the need for autonomy is the man's need to have time to regroup. Some wives complain because their husbands don't immediately talk about their day when they come home from work. They first want to read the paper or water the lawn, anything to clear their mind before engaging in the relationship. It's a male thing. But giving your husband space when he needs it, whether you understand it or not, will gain you a happier husband.

This idea of giving my husband autonomy was a difficult lesson for me to learn. I instinctively wanted to support him in the way that I would want to be supported. If I were in his shoes, for example, I would want to be asked lots of questions about how I was feeling. I would want to be held and pampered. But that's a woman's way, not a man's.

HE NEEDS SHARED ACTIVITY

It was a crisp autumn day when Tom asked Kelly to a Kansas City Chiefs game. "That sounds great! What time?" Kelly said.

They made the date, and Tom smiled after he hung up. This was their third date in the last four weeks, and he was so pleased that she sounded eager to go to a football game.

Tom and Kelly had a great time at the game and took in several more games that same season. They also shopped for cars. Not because either of them needed one. Tom simply enjoyed studying the latest models, and Kelly seemed to enjoy it too. Their relationship was getting more serious, and Tom felt so fortunate to find a woman who enjoyed the same things he did.

By midwinter, Tom was certain Kelly was the woman for him. They got married that spring and both were in bliss. But sometime during their first married year, Kelly's interest in football lessened. She and Tom would sometimes watch the Monday night games, but she never got too excited about attending one. And when Tom suggested that they go to an upcoming automobile show, Kelly begged off.

"I thought you liked looking at cars," Tom complained.

"Oh, honey, I do. I guess I just don't enjoy it as much as you do," Kelly said.

That came as a surprise to Tom. Over the next year, Tom discovered that the things he liked to do and the things Kelly liked to do had little in common. Gradually they arrived at the point where they rarely did much together except go out to dinner once in a while. Tom would have preferred to spend more "fun" time with Kelly, but she seemed quite content to let him do his own thing.

Hurt and bewildered, Tom often wondered why his wife didn't want to be with him.

One of the great gaps between husbands and wives is in their notions of emotional intimacy. If you are like most women, intimacy means sharing secrets, talking things over, cuddling, and so on. But a man builds intimacy differently. He connects by *doing* things together (remember, men focus on achievement). Working in the garden or going to a movie with his wife gives him a feeling of closeness.

> Unless you learn to play a duet in the same key, to the same rhythm, a slow process of disengagement will wedge you apart, first secretly, psychologically, and then openly and miserably.
>
> Walter Wangerin Jr.

Husbands place surprising importance on having their wives as recreational companions. The commercial caricature of men out in the wilderness, cold beer in hand, saying, "It doesn't get any better than this," is false. It can get a lot better than that when a wife joins her husband in a shared activity that he enjoys.

Les recently came home from a speaking engagement in Lake Tahoe. Before he left he was excited because he was going to fly in a day early and do some skiing on his own time. I was so happy for him. He loves to ski—fast—and when we go together I always feel like I am slowing him down. But when he came home from his trip I was shocked by his report: "Well, the powder was great and the weather was perfect, but it's just not the same as skiing with you." Wow! All this time I thought I was a tagalong, and it turns out that he doesn't really enjoy it without me.

Now, I've counseled enough women to know that you might be saying, "What do you do if your activities have little in common?" The answer: Cultivate your spheres of interest. Don't allow you and your partner to drift apart because you can't find something enjoyable to do together. I have seen too many marriages fizzle because a wife didn't use her creative energies to build enjoyable moments of fun and relaxation with her husband. Make a careful list of recreational interests your husband enjoys. Here are a few to get you started: antique collecting, any and all sports, camping, canoeing, table games, puzzles, cooking, dancing, hiking, horseback riding, jogging, moviegoing, ice-skating, sailing, listening to music, swimming, traveling, walking, woodworking, and so on. Your list should be as long as possible. Next, circle those activities that you might find somewhat pleasurable. You can probably find a good half-dozen activities that you can enjoy with your husband. Your next task is to schedule these activities into your recreational time together.

If you learn to meet your husband's need for recreational companionship, you will discover that you are not only husband and wife, but best friends too.

FOR REFLECTION

1. What gender differences can you identify off the top of your head?

2. Can you identify how misunderstandings of gender differences contributed to difficulties in your first marriage? Can you identify how they might affect your current relationship?

3. When it comes to gender differences, most experts today say that the bottom line is not to eliminate them, but to celebrate them. Why?

4. Do you agree that, simplistically speaking, the fundamental difference between the sexes is that men are focused primarily on achievement and women on relationships? What examples can you think of to back up your opinion?

5. Husbands, by and large, don't understand how important emotional intimacy is to their wives. Husbands say, "I want to do things with her, and all she wants to do is talk." Whose problem is this? The husband's, the wife's, or both? How is this misunderstanding related to gender differences?

DO YOU KNOW HOW TO FIGHT A GOOD FIGHT?

The course of true love never did run smooth.

SHAKESPEARE

I have a brain, you know!" I yelled.

"I'm trying to help you, if you'd let me," Les replied.

Our voices seemed to echo through the entire city of San Francisco, where we were on a weekend trip with our friends Randy and Pam. We were trying to catch a streetcar when one of our most explosive conflicts erupted.

It was our third attempt to jump onto a crowded trolley as it reached the crest of a hill. Les, with me holding on to his arm, leaped first to secure a position, but I, for the third time now, pulled back at the last moment.

"This is crazy!" I shouted.

"Just trust me, I know what I'm doing," Les coaxed.

The tension was palpable. Randy and Pam, watching the argument from its inception, stood still. Eventually, in their embarrassment, they crossed the street to escape our hollering.

"Why won't you just trust me?" Les demanded.

As the entire group of moving trolley passengers craned their heads to watch this marital match, I offered a retort that has since become infamous in our household: "I trust God for my safety, but I can't trust you!"

We seem to have our biggest arguments in public. On another occasion we were late for a weekend marriage retreat—and *we* were the speakers. Leslie was still in her office pulling together some last-minute materials, and I was waiting impatiently in the car.

"Okay, Parrott, don't lose it," I murmured to myself. "She'll be out any minute now. Just relax and don't get angry at her." Five minutes turned into fifteen. "Here she comes, just bite your tongue."

It was raining lightly as Leslie climbed into the car. But as she reached to close the car door, her armful of notes and hundreds of handouts slipped away, some into a curbside puddle, most scattering across the wet street.

I couldn't contain myself. "That's it," I said sternly. "I can't believe this! What are we going to do now? Couldn't you see that—"

> Marriage is one long conversation, chequered by disputes.
>
> Robert Louis Stevenson

"You're the one that wanted to do this retreat," Leslie interrupted.

"Oh, don't give me that. You—" My raised voice suddenly stopped as I tried to swallow my sentence. With the car door swung open wide and papers flying everywhere, I suddenly realized our derogatory remarks were being heard by several colleagues who were passing by. Keeping their eyes straight ahead, they pretended not to notice the "marriage experts" having their tiff, but there was no denying that the Parrotts were having a blowup. As we said, we have a knack for doing our "best" fighting in public.

Misunderstanding is a natural part of marriage. No matter how deeply a man and woman love each other, they will eventually have conflict. It is simply unrealistic to expect that both people will always want the same thing at the same time. Conflict in marriage is inevitable.

And when it comes to conflict in second marriages—especially where blending a family is involved — conflict can easily hover over a couple who hasn't learned to manage it. Tina and Scott experienced this. Both had kids from their first marriages, and Scott's sixteen-year-old son, who had recently received his driver's license, was the oldest. So Scott thought it was only natural for his son to use his new mom's automobile to run a few errands. He thought that offering Tina's car to his son was a great way to help them build a bond. Tina, however, didn't see it that way at all. "That car is just about the only thing of monetary value I got from my ex-husband, and I don't want a teenager driving it," she declared. Needless to say, conflict erupted. It was just one of countless conflicts this couple faced.

If you've been married before, you know what we're talking about. If you haven't, you'll understand sooner than you'd like. Thirty-seven percent of newlyweds admit to being more critical of their mates after being married. And 30 percent report an increase in arguments.[1] Stressed-out, dual-career couples today have more to negotiate than ever, and the potential for conflict is at every turn — especially when stepchildren are involved. But for couples who know how to work it out, conflict can actually lead to a deepening sense of intimacy. The trick is knowing *how* to argue.

Let's make this perfectly clear: *Knowing how to fight fair is critical to your survival as a happy couple.* Love itself is not enough to sustain a relationship in the jungle of modern life. Being in love is, in fact, a very poor indicator of which couples will stay married. Far more important to the survival of a marriage, research shows, is how well couples handle disagreements.[2] Many couples don't know how to handle conflict. Some mistake calmness and quiet for marital harmony and go out of their way to smooth over differences without really resolving them. Others, having watched their parents explode at each other, learn the wrong ways of fighting, and their arguments quickly degenerate into insults and abuse.

In this chapter we will show you how to fight fair and reduce your toxic quarrel quotient. We will begin our "combat training" by exploring the common issues that trip up couples. Then we will highlight the four lethal conflict styles you should stay clear of. Next we will tell you why fighting can be good for your marriage, and finally we will give you the rules for fighting a good fight.

WHAT COUPLES FIGHT ABOUT

So what are the thorny issues that cause couples to battle each other? Money? Sex? In-laws? Not always. It generally takes very little for the fur to fly in most marriages. It's the minor, almost embarrassing problems that tear at the fabric of a marriage.

Three days into their honeymoon, Alec and Cindy were ready to pack up and go home. Both had been in a previous marriage, so they knew very well that conflict goes part and parcel with marriage. But for reasons they still don't understand, they began to get on each other's nerves right from the beginning. Instead of unwinding and enjoying each other's company as they started their new life together, they spent all their time fighting. He got sand all over the bottle of sunscreen; she wanted to sit on the beach, and he wanted to stay by the pool; she took too long getting ready to go out in the evening. When Alec and Cindy arrived home a week later, both agreed that their honeymoon was not what either imagined it should be. Why? Because they argued about deep-felt issues? No. They simply bickered about things that didn't really matter. Thankfully, Alec and Cindy realized they both needed to brush up on their conflict management skills, and they soon set a new tone for their marriage. But their honeymoon serves as a reminder to all of us that couples can often fight about trivial issues.

> I would like to have engraved inside every wedding band "Be kind to one another." This is the Golden Rule of Marriage and the secret of making love last through the years.
>
> Randolph Ray

160

The fact that most conflicts erupt over relatively minor matters, however, doesn't diminish the major ones. It seems there is a universal red alert that sounds in every marriage when certain topics are broached. Both happy and unhappy couples struggle with the same topics (although the struggles differ greatly in intensity and frequency).[3]

When it comes to the "big issue" list, research shows that money outranks all other topics as the number one area of conflict among married couples—even for couples in their second marriages.[4] Why? Because couples often have differing money styles, one being a saver and the other a spender. Some bring financial debt into the relationship. All carry some kind of financial fear.—And couples are constantly faced with financial decisions that cause them to ask, "Whose money is it?" This comes as no surprise to couples who are remarrying and trying their best to be equitable with kids in a blended family. It only takes a little experience to know that this can be dicey. What's surprising to many couples is that money fights are not a function of how much money they have or don't have. Couples fight about money no matter what their income is. Some couples argue over whether to go to Barbados or Europe for their vacation; other couples fight over whether they can afford a vacation at all.

Higher incomes can reduce stress, but they don't stop the fighting. Most -couples, regardless of income, have conflicting spending and saving styles. One will be the big spender, the other will be the penny-pincher. Talking openly about money matters is probably the most difficult problem you and your partner will resolve.[5] In fact, a recent survey of more than one thousand married adults found that 32 percent of them said money was the most important issue for couples to discuss prior to getting married.[6] That's why we have devoted a special exercise in the workbook to help you get very practical about setting up a budget, saving together, paying bills, exploring spending styles, and all those other financial matters.

Workbook Exercise 20
Money Talks and So Can We

"Money is the opposite of the weather," someone said. "Nobody talks about it, but everybody does something about it." This exercise, *Money Talks and So Can We*, will not only ensure that you talk about money together, but it will ensure that how you handle your money as a -couple will be wise and profitable.

SYMBIS Report Page 6
What's Your Money Matrix?

Have you explored each other's financial skills, attitudes, and history? It's a personal topic, we know. That's why we've built a personalized money matrix right into the SYMBIS Assessment.

If you're using the assessment, you'll not only uncover each other's money styles but your financial fears and desires. A personalized money talk is sure to minimize financial friction in your marriage, and your personalized report will help in doing just that.

Higher incomes can reduce stress, but they don't stop the fighting. Most couples, regardless of income, have conflicting spending and saving styles. One will be the big spender, the other will be the penny-pincher. Talking openly about money matters is probably the most difficult problem you and your partner will resolve. A good way to start is to discuss your spending styles with each other. How did your childhoods shape your beliefs about money? What are your spending priorities? Are they in sync with your partner's? Don't be disturbed if you find they conflict. The goal here is to compromise. If you let go of right-or-wrong thinking, it will be a lot easier to give and take.

Workbook Exercise 21
Identifying Your Hot Topics

Knowing what pushes your buttons can help you and your partner take special care when it comes to those issues. Many couples feel they are always walking in a minefield, never knowing exactly what sets their mates off. The workbook exercise *Identifying Your Hot Topics* will help you and your partner identify potential trouble spots so you can cope with arguments more effectively.

WHAT UNHAPPY COUPLES DO WRONG

It's a Saturday morning in Seattle. Two newlyweds are finishing their Starbucks coffee while Bach's Brandenburg Concerto No. 4 plays in the background. It is surprisingly sunny, and they find it hard to concentrate on reading the newspaper when they can watch pleasure boats glide by windows that overlook Lake Washington.

But something's different about this idyllic scene. Beneath the couple's casual clothes there are monitors taped to their skin, recording their heart rates. A different gadget measures their perspiration. Their every movement, facial expression, and conversation is being videotaped by three wall-mounted cameras and watched by observers hidden behind one-way glass. Tomorrow they'll have to give blood samples for additional analysis.

This is not a pleasant waterside apartment but a psychology lab at the University of Washington, and these newlyweds are subjects in a study conducted by Dr. John Gottman. Using high-tech equipment, Dr. Gottman and his team of researchers have been studying marriages for more than thirty years, identifying which ones will improve and which ones will deteriorate. They are now able to predict their results with an astounding 95 percent accuracy rate.

Dr. Gottman can spot and track a couple's marital breakdown

by observing how they handle conflict. When four bad omens appear in their conflict—what he calls "The Four Horsemen of the Apocalypse"—danger is imminent, for as each horseman arrives, he paves the way for the next. These four disastrous ways of interacting will sabotage your attempts to resolve conflict constructively. In order of least to most dangerous, they are: (1) criticism, (2) contempt, (3) defensiveness, and (4) stonewalling.[7]

CRITICISM

"I bought a TV for about $200 at a warehouse sale. Molly took one look at it and blew up." Steve was telling us about a recent squabble, and Molly, his wife, was saying how she found herself complaining again and again about Steve's spending habits. Both of them agreed to be thrifty, but they had differing notions of what frugality meant. Steve didn't always turn off the lights when he left a room, for example, while Molly spent hours clipping coupons for their next trip to the grocery store. When Steve didn't measure up to her standards, Molly complained.

> Conflict creates the fire of affects and emotions; and like every fire it has two aspects: that of burning and that of giving light.
>
> Carl Jung

Were Molly's complaints justified? We think so. Not because she is right, but because she has the right to complain. Complaining is a healthy marital activity. Airing a complaint, though rarely pleasant, makes the marriage stronger in the long run than suppressing the complaint.

But Molly, without realizing it, had crossed a dangerous line. As time passed, she found that her comments did not lead Steve to change his spending habits. That's when something potentially damaging to their marriage occurred: Rather than complaining about his *actions*, she began to criticize *him*. "You never carry your weight. You do what you want when you want. It's like living with a grown-up child."

There may not seem to be much difference between complaining and criticizing, but there is. Criticism involves attacking someone's personality rather than his behavior. As a general rule, criticism entails blaming, making a personal attack or an accusation, while a complaint is a negative comment about something you wish were otherwise. Complaints usually begin with the word *I*, and criticisms with the word *you*. For example, "I wish we went out more than we do" is a complaint. "You never take me anywhere" is a criticism. Criticism is just a short hop beyond complaining, and it may seem like splitting hairs, but receiving a criticism really does feel far worse than receiving a complaint.

CONTEMPT

By their first anniversary, Steve and Molly still hadn't resolved their financial differences. In the heat of one particularly nasty argument, Molly found herself shrieking, "Why are you always so irresponsible? You are so selfish!"

Fed up, Steve retorted, "Give me a break. You are so tight you squeak when you walk. I don't know how I ended up with you anyway." The second bad omen, contempt, had entered the scene.

Contempt will poison a relationship whether a couple has been together four months or forty years. What separates contempt from criticism, according to Gottman, "is the *intention to insult* and *psychologically abuse* your partner." There ought to be a law against contempt, because it is aimed right into the heart of a person and ends up destabilizing the relationship and causing pain. When contempt appears, it overwhelms the marriage and blots out every positive feeling partners have for each other. Some of the most common expressions of contempt are name-calling, hostile humor, and mockery. And once they have entered a home, the marriage goes from bad to worse.

DEFENSIVENESS

Once Steve and Molly acted contemptuously, defensiveness entered the picture and made matters worse. They both felt victimized by the other, and neither was willing to take responsibility for setting things right. Who can blame them? If you are being bombarded with insults, the natural inclination is to defend yourself: "It's not my fault. *You* were supposed to pay that bill, not me." One of the reasons defensiveness is so destructive is that it becomes a reflex. The "victim"—reacting instinctively—doesn't see anything wrong with being defensive, but defensiveness tends to escalate a conflict rather than resolve it. Every time either Steve or Molly felt completely righteous in their stance, every time they made excuses and denied responsibility, they added to their marital misery.

> All intimacies are based on differences.
>
> Henry James

STONEWALLING

Steve and Molly were nearing rock bottom. Exhausted and overwhelmed by Molly's attacks, Steve eventually stopped responding, even defensively, to her accusations. "You never say anything," Molly would scream. "You just sit there. It's like talking to a brick wall." Steve usually didn't react at all. On some occasions he would shrug his shoulders, as if to say, "I can't get anywhere with you, so why try?"

Most stonewallers (about 85 percent of them) are men. Feeling overwhelmed by emotions, they start withdrawing by presenting a "stone wall" response. They try to keep their faces immobile, avoid eye contact, hold their necks rigid, and avoid nodding their heads or making the small sounds that would indicate they are listening. Stonewallers often claim they are trying not to make things worse, but they do not seem to realize that stonewalling itself is a very powerful act. It conveys disapproval, icy distance, and smugness.

Stonewalling need not mark the end of a marriage, but once routine interactions have deteriorated to this extent, the marriage will be very fragile and will require a good deal of hard work to save.

Keep in mind that anyone may stonewall or become defensive, contemptuous, or critical. Even with very happy couples these behaviors happen occasionally during an intense marital conflict. The real danger here is letting these ways of interacting become a habit.

Workbook Exercise 22
Mind Reading

Sometimes conflicting couples find common ground only to discover they are standing on quicksand as a result of making incorrect assumptions. The workbook exercise *Mind Reading* will help you and your partner bring your assumptions out into the open.

WHY A GOOD FIGHT AIN'T SO BAD

Conflict is a social taboo, considered morally wrong by some. The assumption that conflict doesn't belong in healthy relationships is based partly on the idea that love is the polar opposite of hate. But emotional intimacy involves feelings of both love and hate, of wanting to be close and needing to be separate, of agreeing and disagreeing.

The absence of fights does not auger well for most marriages. Partners who refuse to accept conflict as a part of marriage miss opportunities to creatively challenge and be challenged by each other. They also risk more negative consequences. Unresolved, unhandled conflict acts as a cancer that erodes the passion, intimacy, and commitment of marriage. Couples who do not "make an issue of things" often resort to "anger substitutes" rather than dealing directly with their emotions. They will overeat, get depressed, gossip, or suffer physical illness. While these substitutes may be more socially accept-able than the direct expression of anger, they can result in what experts call a "devitalized marriage," where false intimacy is the most couples can hope for.[8] A typical evening in the home of a nonfighting couple who has been suppressing anger for years might look like this:

He: *(yawning)* How was your day, dear?
She: *(pleasantly)* Okay, how was yours?
He: Oh, you know, the usual ...
She: Anything special you want to do later?
He: Oh, I don't know ...

Nothing more meaningful is exchanged for the rest of the eve-ning because the energy these two use to repress their anger drains their relationship of vitality. They evade conflict altogether by "gun-nysacking," keeping their grievances secret while tossing them into an imaginary gunnysack that grows heavier and heavier over time. And when marital complaints are toted and nursed along qui-etly in a gunnysack for any length of time, they make a dreadful mess when they burst.

> Love can be angry ... with a kind of anger in which there is no gall, like the dove's and not the raven's.
>
> **Augustine**

The point is that marital conflict is a necessary challenge to be met rather than avoided. We'll say it again: *Conflict is natu-ral in intimate relationships*. Once this is understood, conflict no longer represents a crisis but an opportunity for growth.

David and Vera Mace, prominent marriage counselors, observed that on the day of their wedding, people have three kinds of raw material to work with. First there are the things you have in com-mon, the things you both like. Second are the things in which you are different, but the differences are complementary. And third, there are the differences which are not at all complementary and cause most of your conflict. Every married couple has differences that are not complementary—lots of them. As you and your partner move closer together, those differences become more prominent. You see, conflict can be the result of growing closer together. As we have said to many couples in counseling: Conflict is the price you pay for deepening intimacy. But when you learn to fight fair, your marriage can flourish.

FIGHTING THE GOOD FIGHT

Suppose there were a formula for a happy marriage—would you follow it? Of course, who wouldn't? Especially if the formula were backed up by hard evidence that proved its success.

Well, the astonishing news is that such a formula now exists, thanks to pioneering research done with thousands of couples around the country. Psychologists Howard Markman and Scott Stanley at the University of Denver have predicted, with 80 percent accuracy, who will be divorced six or seven years after marrying. And what they look for is not *whether* a couple argues, but *how* the couple argues.[9]

We now know not only what unhappy couples are doing wrong when they argue, but what happy couples are doing right. Successful couples resolve conflict without leaving scars because they have learned to fight a good fight by sticking closely to the following rules.

DON'T RUN FROM STRIFE

We need to consider the story of the genie in the bottle who, during his first thousand years of incarceration, thinks, "Whoever lets me out will get three wishes," and who, during his second thousand years of incarceration, thinks, "Whoever lets me out I'm gonna kill." Many of us, like that genie, seem to get meaner and more dangerous the longer our grievances are bottled up. Don't allow yourself to bury something that irritates you. Repressed irritations have a high rate of resurrection.

Happy couples may disagree vehemently, but they don't shut their partners out. When one spouse brings up an issue, the other listens attentively. From time to time, the listener will paraphrase what the other says ("You're worried about our overspending?") to make sure the message is understood.

CHOOSE YOUR BATTLES CAREFULLY

Love may be blind, but for many partners marriage is a magnifying glass. Couples who are virtually certain to break up can't seem to find a relaxed, reasonably efficient way of figuring out how to settle differences as small as which movie to see or whose friends to visit. Eventually, their inability to negotiate does them in, no matter how much in love they are. So take the expert's advice and choose your battles carefully.

You've probably seen the "grant me the wisdom to accept the things I cannot change" prayer on plaques and posters. It's overfamiliar, but it's true: One of the major tasks of marriage is learning what can and should be changed (habits of nagging, for example) and what should be overlooked (the way a spouse squeezes the toothpaste tube).

> All married couples should learn the art of battle as they should learn the art of making love. Good battle is objective and honest — never vicious or cruel. Good battle is healthy and constructive, and brings to a marriage the principle of equal partnership.
>
> Ann Landers

We often tell couples that about 90 percent of the issues that they bicker about can probably be overlooked. We know how easy it is to criticize one's mate. We ourselves have done our fair share of yapping about minor infractions, but we've also learned not to sweat the small stuff. This simple advice can keep you from ruining a Friday evening or even an entire vacation. So before you gripe about the way your partner made the bed or cleared the table, ask yourself if it's worth it.

DEFINE THE ISSUE CLEARLY

Shari and Ron seemed addicted to friction. Their most recent blowup occurred while entertaining a group of friends in their home. Everyone was having a good time, enjoying the conversation and the food. As Shari started to serve the dessert, Ron offered to pour the coffee. Shari appreciated his offer and went into the kitchen to get a few more plates. When she returned to the dining room, Ron was still talking and hadn't started serving the coffee. Disgusted, Shari made a derogatory comment, and the two of them began arguing.

"There they go again," said one of the guests.

Embarrassed, Shari and Ron suddenly stopped fighting. After the guests were gone, Shari asked Ron, "Do we fight that frequently?" Ron nodded soberly. Both he and Shari knew they fought too much, but they didn't know why.

Many couples find themselves bickering on a regular basis over just about anything—no issue is too small, or too big, to spar over. When Shari and Ron came to see us, we gave them a simple assignment that reduced the frequency of their arguing almost immediately. It was this: When you feel the tension rising, ask each other to define clearly what the fight is about until both of you understand the issue. Marital battles become habitual if the source of the conflict is not identified, but once couples define the issue, they can be more up front about what is really bugging them. And once the conflict is clearly defined, it often takes care of itself.

At Ron and Shari's dinner fiasco, for example, Shari was not really arguing about having to do all the work herself. She felt angry at Ron for playing basketball earlier in the day when he promised to be home with her, and arguing in front of their friends was a way of getting back at him. Once Ron understood the real issue, he could empathize with Shari's frustration and was better able to repair it.

To identify the real source of a conflict, you must address the questions "What are we really quarreling about?" and "What is the real source of our disagreement?" When couples do not address or cannot answer these questions, the quarrel is often displaced to another topic ("And another thing: Why do you always ...?"). So before you fight, be sure you know what you are fighting about.

STATE YOUR FEELINGS DIRECTLY

Sonia, married just over a year, was continually fighting with her husband about his hectic travel schedule. "I don't understand why your job takes priority over our relationship," she told him over the phone one evening. As he began to explain the pressure of an impending deadline and why he was having to travel so much, it suddenly struck Sonia that she did not really resent him for being gone and working so hard; all she really wanted was for him to say, "I miss you. I feel terrible about not being home. And you're such a fabulous person for being able to handle everything while I'm away." Once she stated her feelings directly, she got what she wanted.

We often teach couples the "X, Y, Z" formula to help them state their feelings. Think of this approach as a kind of game in which you fill in the blanks with your particular gripe in mind: "In situation X, when you do Y, I feel Z." For example, "When you are on the road (X), and you don't tell me that you miss me (Y), I feel unloved and lonely (Z)." Or, "Last Thursday night (X) when you called your mom and talked for a half hour (Y), I felt like our plans for the evening went out the window (Z)." Using this formula will help you avoid insults and character assassination, allowing you instead to simply state how your partner's behavior affects your feelings.

Another example would be, "When we are riding in the car (X) and you change the music without asking me first (Y), I feel hurt that my desires are not considered (Z)." That is far more constructive to your partner than saying, "You never consider my feelings when it comes to music." Although the latter may be what first comes to your mind, it's likely to draw a defensive response that gets you nowhere.

Workbook Exercise 23
Sharing Withholds

For more than ten years of our marriage we have practiced an exercise called "withholds." It is a great way of clearing the deck with your partner on a regular basis so that little conflictual issues don't pile up. The workbook exercise *Sharing Withholds* will help you and your partner stay current with each other on both the negative and positive issues in your relationship.

RATE THE INTENSITY OF YOUR FEELINGS

We have observed that one partner in the couples we counsel is often more expressive than the other. In other words, one person articulates his or her feelings more quickly and more intensely than the other. And we have seen this imbalance cause problems time and again because what is very important to one person may *appear* not to be very important at all.

When James and Karen were setting up their first apartment, Karen wanted to paint the kitchen walls a light blue. She brought home paint samples to show her new husband, but he didn't share her excitement:

"I found the perfect color," Karen said enthusiastically, holding paint chips up to the wall.

"I'm not really crazy about it," Jim said.

"Oh, you'll like it once you see it on the wall. It'll be great."

"I don't know."

The phone rang in the middle of their discussion, and that was the last they talked about it. Three days later, James couldn't believe his eyes when he came home to a light-blue kitchen. "What's this?" he exclaimed. "I thought we agreed not to paint it this color!"

"You said you didn't care, so I went ahead."

"I never said that!"

For the rest of the evening, James and Karen argued over feeling betrayed and unappreciated. But the whole scuffle could have been prevented if they knew just how important (or unimportant) the issue of painting the kitchen was to each of them. As it turned out, James didn't express it well, but he felt very strongly about not painting the kitchen light blue. Karen, on the other hand, was excited and eager to set up house. She could have very easily been talked into another color. Their feelings and how they expressed them were almost polar opposites.

There is a simple technique that could have prevented much of James and Karen's grief. For several years now, we have been handing out hundreds of what we call "Conflict Cards." Using this small plastic card, no bigger than a credit card, helps put couples on even ground when it comes to expressing the intensity of their feelings. We are not sure where the idea for this card came from, but it has helped us resolve plenty of conflicts in our own marriage, and we have seen it work for hundreds of others.

What's on the card? It's simple really. On the card is a scale from one to ten ranking the intensity of a person's feelings:

1. I'm not enthusiastic, but it's no big deal to me.
2. I don't see it the way you do, but I may be wrong.
3. I don't agree, but I can live with it.
4. I don't agree, but I'll let you have your way.
5. I don't agree and cannot remain silent on this.
6. I do not approve, and I need more time.
7. I strongly disapprove and cannot go along with it.
8. I will be so seriously upset I can't predict my reaction.
9. No possible way! If you do, I quit!
10. Over my dead body!

Anytime a heated exchange occurs, a couple can simply pull this list out and rank the depth of their disagreement ("This is a three for me." "It's a five for me."). By rating their conflict, they can play on a level field even when one person is more expressive than the other.

If you would like a free Conflict Card, you can download it free of charge at our website: www.LesandLeslie.com.

By the way, we tell couples who use the Conflict Card that if both partners rank an issue at seven or higher, they should seek objective help from a marriage therapist.

GIVE UP PUT-DOWNS

Remember the childhood saying: "Sticks and stones can break my bones, but names will never hurt me"? That's a lie—names *do* hurt, as many unhappy couples can testify. Unfortunately, couples are generally experts at character assassination ("You don't want a better job because you're lazy").

Put-downs are especially lethal when they attack an Achilles' heel. If your spouse has confessed to you that his cruel high school classmates nicknamed him "egghead," and if, in adulthood, he still has fears about being socially clumsy, that name is off-limits. Two Achilles' heels that are mentioned so often that they must be universal are sexual performance and parents. It is tricky enough, in life's mellowest moments, to discuss sexual dissatisfaction with a mate, but to use it in an argument is a rotten idea. And even though we are allowed to criticize our own parents, it's dirty pool for a spouse to be doing it.

> Do not let the sun go down while you are still angry.
>
> Ephesians 4:26

One of the sad facts of close relationships is that we treat the ones we love worse than we treat just about anyone else. We are more likely to hurl insults at our marriage partner than any other person in our life. We are even more polite to acquaintances than we are to our mates. Here are a few tips for cultivating politeness in your marriage:

- Greet each other with an acknowledgment and warm hello, and mark leaving with a tender good-bye.
- When your partner has done a chore, always show appreciation for the job even if the way it was done doesn't meet with your approval (say, "Thanks for washing the car" rather than, "You missed a spot").
- Surround mealtimes with pleasant conversations. Shut off the gadgets and pay attention to your mate instead.

Research has shown that it takes only one put-down to undo hours of kindness that you give to your partner. So the most gracious offering of politeness you can give your partner is to avoid put-downs altogether.

DON'T DWELL ON DOWNERS

If you are having a fight about how much time your partner is spending at work, we promise you that it will not advance your argument if you also note that he or she is overdrawn at the bank and always leaves you the car with no gas in the tank. Stick closely to the relevant issues—and try to end the fight. Refocus the exchange when it gets off course ("Look, let's just decide who's dropping this off at the dry cleaners. Later we can talk about how the laundry gets done at home."). Try to calm your partner down ("Let's take a break. We're both too upset to discuss this reasonably right now."). Unhappy couples turn every spat into a slippery slope of one unkind word that leads to another:

He: I guess my mistake was looking forward to a nice dinner.
She: If you came home on time, you might have gotten one. You care more about your job than me.
He: Somebody's gotta make a living.
She: It wouldn't be you if I hadn't worked like a dog to put you through school!

This kind of runaway spleen venting is one of the strongest pre-dictors of divorce. These couples veer off into heated, unproductive fighting over tangential or old, unresolved issues. They resolve noth-ing, and negative feelings rage.

In stable marriages, the other partner won't always retaliate when unfairly provoked. Instead, they find ways to defuse tension:

He: I was really looking forward to a decent meal!
She: Your hours are so unpredictable I can't plan one.
He: There's no choice. I'm under a lot of pressure at work.
She: Well, for tonight, should we just order pizza?

It's not how you get into arguments, but how you exit them. If you dwell on downers you will eventually sink.

SYMBIS Report Page 14
Are You Using Conflict to Your Advantage?

Perhaps the quickest and most effective way to keep conflict at bay and "fight a good fight" when it's inevitable, is to step into each other's shoes. That is, accurately understand one another's personality as it relates to handling conflict.

If you're using the assessment, you'll soon see how your distinctive hardwiring can fuel friction or snuff it out. Your personalized report will also provide a customized strategy for successfully managing conflict together — bringing you closer.

Let's face it: All is not fair in love and war. Clean and construc-tive fighting is better than down and dirty fighting, that's for sure. Though of course we are bound to slip, trying to follow the above rules will help you fight a good fight.

FOR REFLECTION

1. What do you typically do when faced with an interpersonal conflict? What works and what doesn't work for you? And what have you learned about marital conflict from your previous marriage?

2. Have you ever noticed any particular "signs" that can alert you to mounting tension before it erupts? For example, does your heart race, do you get sweaty palms, do you avoid eye contact? What might tip you off to the fact that you are about to get upset?

3. Consider the things you and your partner sometimes argue about. What patterns can you detect? Do you see any themes? Do the same issues return again and again?

4. On a continuum with "denial of conflict" on one end and "confrontational" on the other, where would you place yourself? Where would you place your partner? How might your differences affect your arguments?

5. What can you do to avoid the common mistake of turning your complaining into criticism? Why is it important to avoid this pitfall?

6. What do you think about the statement: "Conflict is the price we pay for deepening intimacy"? How would you explain this concept to another person?

7. What did you learn from your parents about handling conflict? Consider behaviors like yelling, blaming, pouting, sarcasm, avoidance, crying, and threatening.

8. One of the reasons money is at the top of the list of things most often argued about is that couples are faced with financial decisions daily. What are some other reasons, in your opinion, that money is so problematic in marriage?

9. When it comes to put-downs, are you clear what is off-limits when arguing with your mate? Does he or she know what is off-limits for you?

10. What is your greatest strength and your greatest challenge, personally, when it comes to fighting a good fight?

11. Every problem you and your mate resolve is part of the confirmation that your marriage will be strong. Take a moment to think of conflicts you have constructively worked through together. What do they tell you about your ability to handle difficult issues as a team?

DO YOU KNOW HOW TO BLEND A FAMILY?

Stepfamilies are the moral pioneers of contemporary family life, showing us all how to love and persevere in the face of loyalties that multiply and divide, but never fully converge.

WILLIAM DOHERTY

"I can't believe you are being so hateful toward me," Cindy complained to her fifteen-year-old daughter, Sarah. "After all we've been through together!"

Cindy and her fiancé, Robert, met with us for premarital counseling sessions in our office. Their wedding was four months off, and they knew they needed help. Not just for the two of them, but also for Cindy's two children from her first marriage, Sarah and Tommy. For this session, they'd brought Sarah and Tommy along.

"You've been through a lot, haven't you?" Les asked as he looked toward Sarah. She simply slouched in her chair, arms tightly crossed, lips pouting, foot wagging furiously. "If you don't feel like talking," Les said, "that's okay."

"You are being so uncooperative," Cindy said to Sarah as Les motioned to Cindy to ease off. But Cindy kept after Sarah. "We're here to help you feel good about my wedding plans."

Sarah rolled her eyes. "You're not letting me invite my friends, so why should *I* even come?" Her nine-year-old brother Tommy nodded supportively but avoided his mother's gaze.

Cindy was on the verge of erupting when Robert jumped in. "Honey, let's slow down here and listen to Sarah." The tension began to gradually lessen as Robert turned to Les with a simple question. "How do we make this family work?"

Like so many simple questions, it did not afford a simple answer. Yet we have heard this question time and time again.

Ray and Julie were asking the very same question. They had just returned from a two-week honeymoon in the Caribbean when Ray's ex-wife announced an engagement to the man she'd been dating for only a few months. That news set off an internal tirade for Ray. Suddenly, he was afraid he was losing his two boys, ages eight and six. "I only see them a few times a month as it is, and they're going to have a new father figure living with them," he confided in us. "So I told my sons that if either one of them referred to their new stepfather as 'Dad,' they would never see me again."

Ray was proud of having stood up for himself, but Les and I were horrified at the message he was sending to his young sons: If you get close to your stepfather, you will lose your biological father. Ray's fear had clouded his judgment.

Ray picked up on our worry. "What's wrong?" he asked.

We expressed concern for his fear and pain, then asked, "How do you think your children felt when you said this to them?"

He soon saw what he had done. He recognized that he had threatened them with the scariest threat possible, that of losing their father forever.

"I didn't mean to scare them," he said as he held back his tears. Julie slid close to him on the sofa and held his hand. Ray tearfully admitted that there was nothing his boys could ever do to make him abandon them. "We just need to know how to make this family, or whatever it is, work."

Stepfamily, secondary family, blended family, combined family, extended family, expanded family, nontraditional family—whatever you call it, it *is* work.[1] And exactly how you work at it can be one of the most important determining factors of whether your marriage will become what you desire. So, we ask you: Do you know how to blend a family?

Maybe both of you are entering this marriage with a set of kids. Perhaps one of you has children and the other does not. Or, maybe one of you has kids who visit you only two weekends a month. About 65 percent of remarriages involve children from a prior marriage. Whatever your situation with children in your new marriage, we dedicate this chapter to giving you tools for building a marriage — and a family — that withstands the predictable jostles and jolts you are bound to encounter.

> Love builds bridges where there are none.
>
> R. H. Delaney

We begin with a word to your specific situation, as a spouse who is bringing children into your marriage or as a spouse who is marrying into a family situation. We then give the remainder of the chapter over to the best advice we've gleaned from other experts and couples who have walked this path before you. We think you'll find their ideas to be especially helpful.

IF YOU ARE THE BIOLOGICAL PARENT

Cindy (from the opening of this chapter) had dated a few times since her divorce some ten years ago, but nothing serious ever evolved until Robert. He was the first person with real marriage potential. Not only that, her kids liked him. That's why it was so puzzling to Cindy that they were not excited about her wedding. In time, she learned what was going on for them. While they both liked Robert, they did not like the way Cindy treated them around him. And the more Cindy insisted on the way they should behave toward him, the more upset the children became.

"Robert's okay," Sarah confessed. "I just don't like who my mom has become since she's been with him. Every day she gets more bossy."

Cindy bristled at this news, but eventually she came to see that she did treat them differently around Robert. This insight gave her an opportunity to change this new behavior she didn't even know existed until they pointed it out to her.

This lack of awareness, coupled with disgruntled kids, is a common occurrence for parents who are getting married a second time and bringing their kids into the relationship with them. And if you fall into this category, you probably know how Cindy felt. After all, you're not just getting married to a person; you and your kids are joining this person to create a new kind of family unit. That's a big step. Perhaps the biggest you will ever take. So it stands to reason that there may be some anxiety that seeps into your situation. And while there are no cure-alls for alleviating such anxiety completely, there are several things you can do that will improve your entry into this new world.

COMPLETE YOUR UNFINISHED BUSINESS

To begin with, it is critically important that you complete the proverbial unfinished business from your first marriage if you want success in your second. Whether your first marriage ended in divorce or in death, it is crucial to tie up the loose ends of that relationship. Why? Because you will increase the odds of avoiding the same mistakes in your second marriage. As Richard Stuart and Barbara Jacobson state in their book *Second Marriage*, "You can't offer your present partner a fair deal if you haven't come to terms with your past."[2] And coming to terms with your first marriage means remembering that both you and your partner contributed to both the bad and the good in the marriage.

Workbook Exercise 24
Creating a Clean Slate

If love the second time around is ever to succeed, it will be because you've done your best to come to terms with your first marriage and create a clean slate for your second. This workbook exercise will help you do just that. If this is your first marriage but your partner's second, we encourage you to discuss your partner's results after he or she has a chance to complete the exercise alone.

BE CIVIL TO YOUR EX

How you conduct yourself around your ex-spouse will be a living lesson to your children. After all, the home they grow up in is their university of relationships. It is here that they learn how relationships work, and you are their primary instructor. So, the more civil you can be toward your ex, the more civil your children will be in general.

Another important point to keep in mind is that your ex-spouse is still a vital part of your children's lives. Children need to be allowed to have memories of their other parent. They need to have pictures of him or her and time to enjoy outings together and regular visits. If your new spouse doesn't accept this very well, it is your job as the biological parent to help out by allowing the child time to recall past experiences. Research shows that the children who adjust the best to divorce are those who have the easiest access to both their parents.[3] This means they can talk to, write to, and/or see their nonresidential parent as often as possible. It

> Every major change in life involves some degree of loss. Seldom is the loss as great as when a man or woman is widowed or goes through a divorce.
>
> Frederick Flach

185

means they feel free to love the other biological parent. Children who are asked to choose between biological parents are put in a no-win emotional dilemma that is plainly unfair to the child. Children in this situation have enough to contend with without having to choose one parent over the other. So if your children visit your ex-spouse on occasion, remember that the ability to adjust to two sets of rules or two ways of doing things from two different households is possible as long as they are not asked to choose which is better.

BE THE PRIMARY DISCIPLINARIAN

Discipline is another issue for biological parents. Experts recommend that at the beginning of your second marriage, discipline should come primarily from you. This doesn't mean you choose all the rules, however. You and your new spouse should decide on the rules together, but you should be the one to talk to your kids about the rules of your new home, and you should enforce the consequences. Later, after relationships have developed, your new spouse can become more involved. By the way, this delineation of discipline doesn't mean the children's new stepparent doesn't parent right from the beginning. The stepparent should help nurture your children, transmit your shared values, give positive strokes, and set appropriate limits on their behavior ("You can play after the dishes are done").[4] By discipline, we mean the process of enforcing consequences through punishment when a child disobeys a parent's rule or instruction.

> Don't worry that children never listen to you; worry that they are always watching you.
>
> Robert Fulghum

This distinction between discipline and parenting brings up an important question: What do you do when the biological parent isn't at home but the discipline is needed? Stepfamily expert Ron Deal says, "Live on borrowed power—just like babysitters." In other words, when parents leave their children with a babysitter, they generally instruct the children that "she is in charge while Mommy and Daddy are gone." Power is passed to the babysitter by the parent, and the children understand that to disobey her is to disobey them. The same dynamic works with stepparents. The biological parent must make it clear to the children that the stepparent is an extension of the biological parent and disobeying them is to disobey the biological parent. This gives stepparents temporary power to uphold rules and enforce consequences that have already been communicated to the children by the biological parent. Later, the biological parent can return home and reinforce the stepparent's borrowed authority with a word of support for the stepparent in front of the children. In time, as stepparents and children form their own bond, stepparents can begin standing on their own authority.

HAVE EMPATHY FOR YOUR SPOUSE IN THE STEPPARENT ROLE

Here's another important note for you, as the biological parent: Your new partner, if he or she does not already have children, is not only becoming a spouse, but a parent as well. He or she may feel thrust into the role of "instant parent" with little or no practical experience. They are being asked to play a knowledgeable role as parent in your household when they do not have the benefit of growing into the role as you did. Stepparents are often expected to adjust instantly as though parenting is an inborn skill. It isn't. Biological parents have a huge advantage because they are innately more tolerant of their children's personalities and behaviors than someone who doesn't know them so well.[5] A stepparent may also be anxious that he or she can never be as good a parent as the previous partner. You can help your new spouse by helping him or her get to know your children. Show your new spouse photo albums and tell family stories that help fill in the texture of each child's history. Most of all, remember to be patient with your new spouse as he or she learns to love your children and to become an effective parent with them.

One final thought. Realize that your new spouse's lack of history with your children provides your spouse with an objective perspective on your children's personality and behavior that you do not have. Don't be too quick to disqualify their perspective or suggestions. They may see what your blind spots won't allow you to see.

IF YOU ARE THE STEPPARENT

Unfortunately, stepparents have gotten a bad rap. With the unflattering stories of wicked stepmothers in *Cinderella*, *Hansel and Gretel*, and *Snow White*, or the "wicked stepfather" of Dickens's *David Copperfield* or Shakespeare's *Hamlet*, stepparents often start out with an unfair disadvantage—at least with any literate child. But this disadvantage cannot rest solely on fiction. After all, bringing up someone else's child—and that is what it means to be a stepparent—is no small task. Sure, it can be rewarding and stimulating. But it can be deflating and exhausting too. No matter how close your relationship, you do not have the biological link that brings with it an unquestioning commitment to love a child no matter what he or she does—and that same commitment is missing on the other side of the equation with the child you are stepparenting. Without this biological link it can be extremely difficult to tolerate, let alone like, a stepchild who is being particularly tiresome, and coping with a headstrong teenager you're not biologically related to can be a nightmare.

> Love and marriage may go together like a horse and carriage, but love and remarriage aren't as neatly complementary. The carriage may be so crowded that the horse has trouble pulling it.
>
> Susan Kelley

As a stepparent, you may feel that you are out on a grafted limb at times, excluded from the biological link that your partner has with the children. And because of this, you may feel unable to play a full parental role. Clearly a great many stepparents do have warm and loving relationships with their stepchildren and a strong commitment to them, but this is a condition you can't take for granted. The following words of advice are offered in the hope that you will rarely feel out on the lonely limb of stepparenting.

DON'T TRY TO REPLACE THE MISSING PARENT

First and foremost, don't try to replace a biological parent. Just in case you forget that you're not the "real" parent, your stepchild will remind you with the standard stepchild refrain: "I don't have to mind you! You're not my real mother (father)!" You can be your own kind of parent, but you can't replace a parent that your stepchild loves. So don't try to fit into a parenting mold that you don't fit; instead be who you are and pay attention to ways that you can develop your own unique and healthy relationship with the children of your new spouse.

> Have courage for the great sorrows of life and patience for the small ones; and when you have laboriously accomplished your daily task, go to sleep in peace. God is awake.
>
> Victor Hugo

TAKE A COURSE IN PARENTING

If you have no children of your own, we urge you to take a crash course in parenting. By this we mean talk to other parents, or better yet, other stepparents who have a successful track record. Read a book or two on parenting that comes highly recommended. Subscribe to a parenting magazine. Attend a stepparenting seminar at a local school or church. In other words, take your preparation for being a new parent as seriously as you do your preparation for being a new spouse. You have begun a major undertaking, and the more equipped you are, the easier your life and the stronger your marriage will be.

START SLOW

As you are settling into your new role as a spouse and a step-parent, take on your parenting role very slowly. You will need to build relationships with your stepchildren before attempting to set disciplinary limits for them. With teens, by the way, a disciplinary type of interaction may never be achieved. Talk to your spouse to be sure he or she as the biological parent is taking the primary role with discipline. As your relationship with the children becomes more comfortable, you may be able to gradually take on more of the traditional parenting role with discipline. Grow into your role, and let your stepchildren set the pace for the relationship. Let them determine the amount of affection shown, the terms they use to refer to you and your family (as long as they are respectful), and the level of authority they grant you. In the meantime, focus on sending positive signals to the children through your words and actions. Maybe a kiss or hug isn't comfortable at this time, but a hand on the shoulder can say, "I care about you." Praise will also make the child feel better about himself and will encourage him to do what you ask.

DON'T FRET ABOUT THE EX

Another important point to remember is to not waste precious time and energy by obsessing about your partner's ex-spouse. The more you think about him or her, the less effective you'll be as a stepparent. If you have to discuss the ex-spouse every day, or most days out of the week, then it's time to take an honest assessment of your situation and make a change. Even if you're one of the unfortunate people who have a "crazy ex" to deal with, you must force yourself not to play the game. If there are legal issues, let your spouse's lawyer deal with it. If the ex-wife calls on the phone to whine, don't answer when she calls. Games only work if everyone is participating. So if your partner's ex-spouse can no longer push your buttons, he or she will quit trying. The point is to not spend your time and energy on him or her. To do so will only make matters worse, undermining your ability to be an effective stepparent. Stay away from the ex-spouse not only for the children, but for the sake of your new marriage too.

THE EX AND PHONE ETIQUETTE

One more thing along these lines is worth mentioning. This may seem like a small detail, but it is so common we feel compelled to mention it. Don't tell your new spouse what to say while he or she is on the phone with the ex-spouse. It may be difficult to sit there and say nothing when you think your spouse is getting taken advantage of, but passing notes to him or her about what to say to the ex while they're talking on the phone is sure to backfire. First, you really cannot hear the other side of the conversation, and second, this is going to irritate your mate and cause problems between the two of you. Don't allow the ex-spouse to have that kind of control. Let your spouse have a conversation without you nosing in. Leave the room. Then when it's done, come in, hug and kiss, and suggest doing something fun. You and your new family will benefit from this.

GIVE YOUR SPOUSE TIME ALONE WITH THE CHILDREN

One final suggestion: Allow your spouse to spend time with his or her children alone. In the beginning it will be easier for everyone if you allow your partner time with the children without you being around. After a while that probably won't be necessary, but at first when the children visit, make yourself scarce unless they invite you along. And they will eventually invite you. Of course, in this process, you don't want to make them think you don't want to be around. Make it clear that you feel they need time alone with their mom or dad, and if anyone needs you, they know where to find you. We mention this, because early in marriage it's common for newlyweds to be clingy and touch in front of the kids. But on occasion, back off and let them sit with their mommy or daddy. Show the children you are not competing for their parent's time or love. They will compete with you for it, but don't get caught fighting that war. Trust and work with your new partner to balance their time and energy between you and the kids. Giving the stepchildren and your spouse your permission to be together without fear of hurting you is nothing short of a gift, although it can feel like a sacrifice. But remember, giving them uninterrupted time provides space for you to develop relationships with them. If you're like many stepfamilies, you do not have the kids all the time, so it's not going to hurt to allow them this time with their biological parent.

> The art of love . . . is largely the art of persistence.
>
> Albert Ellis

LIVING SUCCESSFULLY IN A COMBINED FAMILY

Lisa is a nine-year-old girl who lives with her divorced mother and visits her remarried father whose new wife has two children from her previous marriage. Even when she is home with her mother, it's not the intact family she knew through her early years. Her mother feels more like an older confidante, especially when her mother is in one of her on-again-off-again dating relationships.

When Lisa visits her father it's an entirely different feeling. She has a biological dad mixed with her stepmother, whom she calls "Mom." But here she shifts from being an only child in her biological mother's home to having stepsiblings in the other. Since one of the stepsiblings is older, Lisa also has to adjust to a different birth-order position.

Another thing. Lisa has more than two sets of grandparents—she also has a set of step-grandparents. Now if her mother marries the man she is currently seeing, who happens to have four children from a previous marriage, the complexities of Lisa's family life multiply astronomically.

It's certainly not the traditional family. Yet one third of Americans are stepparents, stepchildren, stepsiblings, or some other member of a stepfamily. And it's easy for any member of such a complex family structure to feel lost, left out, displaced, hurt, and angry. That's why it is crucial for a couple like you who is just beginning to build one of these complex family systems to do everything within your power to combine a family in the healthiest of ways.

We have talked with dozens of stepfamily experts and interviewed countless couples who have successfully navigated the complex waters of combined families. What follows are their top suggestions for steering clear of the rocks and setting your sail for a wonderful family life on board your new marriage.

> Every relationship seems simple at its start. It is free of ties or claim, unburdened by responsibilities, by worry about the future or debts to the past. And then how swiftly the perfect unity is invaded; the relationship changes. It becomes complicated, encumbered by its contact with the world.
>
> Anne Morrow Lindbergh

MAKE THE NEW MARRIAGE THE CENTER OF YOUR FAMILY

Nearly everyone we talked to said the new marriage needed to be the first priority. Stepfamilies are no different from other families in this respect. A child may complain that she has been usurped by Dad's new wife, particularly if she and her dad had a close relationship when they were a single-parent family, but she will eventually discover that her own sense of security is strengthened when the new marriage is strong.

Making his new marriage a priority was difficult for Mike. After feeling like a failure from the dissolution of his first marriage, he was determined to be a successful parent with his three daughters. So in the early months of his second marriage, he began to devote more time and energy to his daughters than to his wife. No matter what the issue, the children came first. He was so focused on them that his wife felt she got only his leftover energy, at best. It didn't take long before their marriage was on the rocks and the kids were feeling more anxious than ever.

Here's the point. As you form a solid bond as a couple, you become better parents together. When couples have a good relationship, they are able to work together on meeting the needs of the children. This reduces the parents' feelings of being caught in the middle between the children and the new partner. It's a win-win for both parents and children.

> The world is round, and the place which may seem like the end may also be only the beginning.
>
> Ivy Baker Priest

BUILD NEW FAMILY TRADITIONS AND ACTIVITIES WHILE RESPECTING THE OLD ONES

Every family has a narrative that is made up of traditions and activities unique to them. One family plays a board game after dinner each night. Another enjoys their boat on the weekends. These family activities make up the memories and the stories of their shared life as a family. And they are critically important.

As you try to blend different backgrounds, histories, and lifestyles in your combined family, conflicts are sure to arise. It's only natural. But as you forge ahead and develop activities and traditions that your new family enjoys together, the conflicts will begin to fade—but only if you allow these activities to be born out of your current relationships, not by forcing something that used to work onto your present family.

Sondra, whose eleven-year-old stepdaughter, Wendy, has lived with her for the past two years, said, "I wish Wendy liked camping and hiking. But she doesn't. Wendy wishes I liked shopping. But I loath it." What's a stepmother and stepdaughter to do? "We accepted our differences," Sondra told us, "and found our common ground elsewhere." Sondra and Wendy cook together. They try out new recipes together and often watch the Food Channel for new ideas. When Sondra and Wendy cook a meal together, it's a family event. Dad sets the table, and Wendy's stepbrother designs a fancy menu on his computer that includes photos from his digital camera.

While still maintaining their differences, this family is beginning to develop their own traditions and are building a history together. A photo album is growing that chronicles their new family traditions.

> Never think that God's delays are God's denials. Hold on; hold fast; hold out. Patience is genius.
>
> Comte de Buffon

HOLD FAMILY MEETINGS

We heard this from nearly every couple and professional we talked to about stepfamilies. Having a set time when the family comes together seems to work wonders for bringing a new family together. It is a time to talk about the schedule for the week and the things that are important to each individual member in the coming days. It is a time to air grievances and plan for an exciting family event, like a vacation.

"Children need a chance to vent their frustrations and know that they will be heard," said one father. "We call it our weekly powwow, and it happens every Sunday night after dinner." In one of their weekly powwows, they decided to buy a dog together. As a family project, they researched different breeds. In the end, they decided to get a dog from the pound. "That process was so bonding," the father told us. "And it would have never happened without our family meetings."

These meetings don't have to be held at a specific place and time. When the atmosphere is relaxed and talk is easy, you can begin tossing ideas back and forth. "For us," said one mother, "that usually happens in one of two places: around the dinner table, when we don't have to rush off to a ball game or some other activity, and on a long car drive."

Find your own way, carve out your own pathway for these meetings, but give them a try. Create a forum where everyone gets a chance to say how he or she thinks things should be done. As your kids discuss such things as curfews, chores, and allowances, and as you all create an exciting event to look forward to, you will sense deeper connections beginning to grow. You will discover a more cooperative spirit for having worked out a plan together.

PROVIDE PERSONAL SPACE FOR EVERYONE

This is particularly true if you have a child who visits on occasion. While your home may not allow you to have an entire bedroom for a child who is only with you every other weekend, this child still needs a space of her own, a special spot in your household.

Five-year-old Emily eagerly anticipates sharing her room with her nine-year-old half sister, Susan, on alternate weekends, during school holidays, and for a month in the summer. Even at this young age, Emily understands that one drawer and a small portion of the closet in the room are not hers. They belong exclusively to Susan. And Susan knows that the clothes, books, and games which she leaves behind will be untouched when she returns.

> We all have big changes in our lives that are more or less a second chance.
>
> Harrison Ford

With no drawer or desk or bed, it is not possible to feel as though you belong. Even a shelf of your own or a portion of the family bulletin board gives you a claim in the house. And once that space is designated for the child, remember to refer to it as that child's. As one ten-year-old we talked to put it, "Why can't they say, 'This is Aaron's room which we use for a study when he's not here,' rather than 'This is our study which Aaron uses when he's here'?"

DON'T RUSH INTO HAVING YOUR OWN CHILD TOGETHER

Once again, we hear this advice again and again. Experts and couples alike told us that, while it is tempting for couples in a second marriage to want to have their own child together right away, this is something that needs to be given plenty of time.

Statistics show that women entering a marriage with a man who already has children often have another child within two years of their marriage. It is normal to want to have your own children to further your bond with your new spouse. However, it is far better to allow the entire family to adjust before bringing more children into the situation. Most experts say you should consider giving your marriage at least three years before bringing more children into it.

Another reason for the wait is a discouraging statistic that experts point to: Most second marriages that fail do so within two years of the woman giving birth. There is no doubt that stepchildren, financial problems, and unresolved issues with ex-spouses are all important issues that contribute to the high divorce rate among second marriages. So take your time. Allow everyone in the new family to adjust to the myriad of new dynamics before you even think about having a baby.

Workbook Exercise 25
Remarried with Children

Now that you have explored the various bits of advice other successful couples and experts have for people in your shoes, it's time to put the advice into practice. How are you going to devise your own plan for combining your new family in the healthiest ways? This workbook exercise will help you answer that question.

DEALING WITH EXTENDED FAMILY

Every marriage—whether it be the first, second, or third—involves more than the bride and groom. In fact, we know some ministers who will actually have the two extended families present at a wedding ceremony and ask if they take each other as part of a new family to support this new marriage. While that may be a little extraordinary for most, all would agree that you are not just marrying your soul mate, you are bringing his or her parents and grandparents, as well as siblings, into this new relationship. Of course, in a second marriage you may also be bringing children into the mix from both sides, and that impacts grandparents and maybe even great-grandparents. For this reason, it is imperative that you explore the dynamics of these relationships with your new spouse. Take time to introduce your new spouse to each of your extended family members. Help them get a feel for who each one of them is and how a positive relationship can be cultivated with their varying personalities. Paint a picture of your family history and provide opportunities for them to get to know your new spouse. The stronger these relationships with extended family members, the stronger your marriage.

MAKING SENSE WITH MONEY MATTERS

Money, as we pointed out earlier, is the number one source of conflict in marriage. And when it comes to second marriages, the potential for the fur to fly over financial issues is even stronger. Why? Because there may be houses to sell, alimony issues, inheritances, debt on one side or the other, and so on. The point is that money matters in second marriages are complicated. Very complicated. You will be deciding important issues like whether to have separate bank accounts, how your money gets spent, whether you work with a budget, how to save for retirement, whether children get an allowance and how much, which house will you live in, and so on. Of course, all this will be influenced by your previous marriage and how money was—or wasn't—handled. You may also be wondering about prenuptial agreements (something we typically do not support since it presupposes a dissolution of the marriage). We don't know what your specific money issues are as you blend your new family, but we do know that money matters have potential to cause great pain if they are not dealt with properly. So take the time to explore them thoroughly. Study your options together. You may find it helpful to tap into the resources of an expert like Dave Ramsey. You may even want to consult a financial planner who has experience with blended families.

TWO FINAL WORDS FOR STEPFAMILIES

We hope you know that this chapter is truly just the tip of the iceberg when it comes to information on stepfamilies.[6] Researchers are learning more each day to help improve the life of stepfamilies. But as new information expands our knowledge, one thing remains certain. Even so-called "normal" intact families have difficulties. Children play one parent against the other, for example, and cause chaos in their parents' lives. Parents all over the world have trouble finding time to be alone with each other, and so on. Your situation as a stepfamily will be no different. Difficulties are normal. And remember this: It takes at least three years for a combined family to start acting like a family. *Practice patience.*

SYMBIS Report Page 7A
Ready for Life in a Blender?

Having new family as parents along with your new marriage requires plenty of discussion. If you're using the SYMBIS Assessment, you'll discover personalized topics that will be worthy of exploration.

FOR REFLECTION

1. If you are the biological parent, what is one specific thing you can do to improve the blending process? Is there anything about your personal situation that will make blending your family more difficult?

2. Discipline is a big issue in blended families. If you are the biological parent, how can you take some concrete steps to be the primary disciplinarian?

3. If you are the stepparent, what is one specific thing you can do to improve the blending process?

4. As a stepparent it can sometimes be tough to give your spouse time alone with his or her biological children. What can you do to feel good about this and ensure that it happens?

5. Consider building new family traditions and activities into your blended family. What might they be? How can you respect the old traditions while building new ones?

ARE YOU AND YOUR PARTNER SOUL MATES?

. . . and the two will become one flesh.
Ephesians 5:31

"We are exactly alike," John blurted out. He and Nancy were one of a dozen newly married couples we were teaching. I (Leslie) had just asked each of them to talk about their differences when John made his proud exclamation. The other couples looked dismayed.

Les, as any psychologist would do, said, "Tell us about that, John."

Nancy nodded as her new husband replied, "We just don't have any big differences, that's all. We like all the same things and never disagree."

"Wow," Les said with a tinge of sarcasm in his voice. I felt myself starting to cringe, knowing what Les was thinking and hoping he wouldn't say it. But he did. "You are the first couple I have ever met that is exactly the same."

The class giggled, and John rolled his eyes. "Well, we are not *exactly* the same," he admitted.

Some couples strain to duplicate each other in order to cover up their differences. Newlyweds, for example, often force an unrealistic similarity upon their tastes, opinions, priorities, and habits. They do so with the best of intentions, but their sameness is no more real than

Adam and Eve's when they covered their differences with fig leaves. God created each person to be different, and to deny that uniqueness leads only to pretense, not partnership.

Another member of the same small group said, "Sharon and I have a fifty-fifty marriage, half and half." Other couples agreed. Sharing the load, even-steven, is a much better way to create oneness, they believed. "Yeah," said Sharon, "but sometimes our halves don't always fit together."

> Whoever said marriage is a fifty-fifty proposition laid the foundation for more divorce fees than any short sentence in our language.
>
> **Austin Elliot**

She's right. A "fifty-fifty marriage" only works if each partner is a fraction. But we aren't. Each of us is a whole person. We don't subtract something from ourselves when we get married. We remain whole and we want to be loved as a whole, not cut to fit together.

We have seen couples try to build a marriage on the fifty-fifty principle, taking turns deciding this and that, splitting resources, weighing portions, counting privileges. But we have yet to find a fifty-fifty couple who doesn't feel that taking turns is cheating them out of their presumed rights. Often the more strong-willed partner, consciously or unconsciously, wields the knife that divides the "halves," and one half becomes "more equal" than the other.

So how then do a man and a woman become one in marriage? To put it another way: How do a man and a woman become soul mates? The answer is found exactly where you might suspect—deep in the soul. Recently, scientific research has backed up what common sense has been telling us for years; mainly, that tending to the spiritual dimension of marriage is what unites couples in unbreakable bonds.[1] Marriage thrives when its soul is nourished.

In this chapter we explore the most important and least-talked-about aspect of a healthy marriage—the spiritual dimension. We begin by exploring the need for spiritual intimacy and its deep meaning to your marriage. Next we show how God is revealed in your partnership and how marriage is closer to the nature of God than any other aspect of life. Then we outline some specific and practical tools for tending to the soul of your marriage. We conclude this chapter with a final remembrance.

SYMBIS Report Page 15
When Do Each of You Feel Closest to God?

Each of you is prone to walk a unique pathway to God. You are each likely to lean into certain spiritual practices that you don't necessarily share — even if you are both sincere and passionate about your faith.

Your SYMBIS Assessment spells out your differing spiritual pathways and how you can join them together as you make your journey toward becoming soul mates.

SPIRITUAL INTIMACY: THE ULTIMATE MEANING OF MARRIAGE

On February 12, 1944, thirteen-year-old Anne Frank wrote the following words in her now-famous diary:

> Today the sun is shining, the sky is a deep blue, there is a lovely breeze and I am longing—so longing for everything. To talk, for freedom, for friends, to be alone.
>
> And I do so long ... to cry! I feel as if I am going to burst, and I know that it would get better with crying, but I can't, I'm restless, I go from room to room, breathe through the crack of a closed window, feel my heart beating, as if it is saying, can't you satisfy my longing at last?
>
> I believe that it is spring within me, I feel that spring is

awakening, I feel it in my whole body and soul. It is an effort to behave normally. I feel utterly confused. I don't know what to read, what to write, what to do, I only know that I am longing.[2]

There is in all of us, at the very center of our lives, a tension, an aching, a burning in the heart that is deep and insatiable. Most often it is a longing without a clear name or focus, an aching that cannot be clearly pinpointed or described. Like Anne Frank, we only know that we are restless, aching deep within our soul.

Most people expect marriage to quench their soulful longing, and it often does for a time. But for many, the deep, restless aching echoes again. It certainly did for Ryan and Ashley. They did everything they could to stack the odds for a strong marriage in their favor. They went through premarital counseling, adjusted faulty expectations, learned how to communicate effectively, practiced conflict resolution, and so on. They read books about marriage, attended seminars, and even had an older couple who agreed to mentor them during their first married year. Ryan and Ashley took marriage seriously and their efforts were paying off—at least for the time being. They were now in their tenth year of marriage and, from all appearances, doing well. But in spite of all their effort, something was missing.

> We can now recognize that the fate of the soul is the fate of the social order; that if the spirit within us withers, so too will all the world we build about us.
>
> Theodore Roszak

"We are very much in love," Ashley told us, "but sometimes it feels like we are just going through the motions."

"Yeah," said Ryan. "We are definitely in love, but sometimes the relationship feels—I don't know—empty, I guess. Like there should be a deeper connection."

Ryan and Ashley, in many respects, were a model couple. They did all the things healthy couples do. They were psychologically astute, emotionally balanced, and kept their relationship in working order. But their hearts continued to be restless, longing for something more, something deeper. Ryan and Ashley, knowingly or not, were yearning to be soul mates.

What Ryan and Ashley still needed to learn was that there is more to a thriving marriage than good communication, conflict resolution, and positive attitudes. While each of these tools is critically important for a lasting and meaningful relationship, they are not sufficient. Marriage is not a machine that needs routine maintenance to keep it functioning, but a supernatural event founded upon a mutual exchange of holy pledges. Above all, marriage is a deep, mysterious, and unfathomable endeavor.

Even happily married couples like Ryan and Ashley eventually discover an innate longing to bond with their lover, not just for comfort, not just for passion—but also for *meaning*. Our lives go on day after day. They may be successful or unsuccessful, full of pleasure or full of worry. But do they *mean* anything? Only our soul can answer.

For married couples, spiritual meaning should be a shared pursuit.[3] While every individual must come to an understanding of life's meaning alone, couples must also discover the meaning of their marriage together. You are not just husband and wife. You have given birth to a marriage that is very much like a living being, born from you both. And the soul of your new marriage needs nourishment.

Sharing life's ultimate meaning with another person is the spiritual call of soul mates, and every couple must answer that call or risk a stunted, underdeveloped marriage. Like yeast in a loaf of bread, spirituality will ultimately determine whether your marriage rises successfully or falls disappointingly flat.

The spiritual dimension of marriage is a practical source of food for marital growth and health. No single factor does more to cultivate oneness and a meaningful sense of purpose in marriage than a shared commitment to spiritual discovery. It is the ultimate hunger of our souls.

Workbook Exercise 26
Your Spiritual Journey

Each person brings to a marriage his or her own spiritual quest. The workbook exercise *Your Spiritual Journey* will help you and your partner share your spiritual walks.

FINDING GOD IN YOUR MARRIAGE

One of the most compelling love stories in our time involves a couple who, in the beginning, lived an ocean apart. He was a scruffy old Oxford bachelor, a Christian apologist, and an author of bestselling books for children. She, an American, was much younger and divorced with two sons.

After first meeting during her visit to England in 1952, C. S. Lewis and Joy Davidson fed their relationship by mail. Intellectual sparks from the minds of each ignited their appreciation and respect for each other. When Joy moved to England with her boys, the relationship enjoyed the benefits of proximity. And when her departure from England seemed imminent because of a lack of funds and an expiring visitor's visa, C. S. Lewis made a decision: If Joy would agree, they would be married.

> Thou hast made us for Thyself, and our hearts are restless till they rest in Thee.
>
> Augustine

Early in the marriage, Joy's body revealed a secret it had kept hidden. She had cancer—and it was irreversible. The well-ordered life of C. S. Lewis suffered a meltdown. But in the process, the English man of letters realized how deep his love for Joy really was.

Moving on with their lives, the Lewises sought and got the added blessing of the church on their marriage, which had originally been formalized in a register's office. They gave Joy the best treatment available. Then he brought her home, committed to her care. It is not surprising that Joy's body responded. However, her remission was short-lived.

Near death, Joy told him, "You have made me happy." Then, a little while after, "I am at peace with God." Joy died at 10:15 that evening in 1960. "She smiled," Lewis later recalled, "but not at me."

If there is a lesson to be gained from this amazing love story, it must be that partners without a spiritual depth of oneness can never compete with the fullness of love that soul mates enjoy.

Marriage, when it is healthy, has a mystical way of revealing God, a way of bringing a smiling peace to our restless hearts.

When researchers examined the characteristics of happy couples who had been married for more than two decades, one of the most important qualities they found was "faith in God and spiritual commitment."[4] Religion, it has been proved, provides couples with a shared sense of values, ideology, and purpose that bolsters their partnership.

> We feasted on love; every mode of it, solemn and merry, romantic and realistic, sometimes as dramatic as a thunderstorm, sometimes comfortable and unemphatic as putting on your soft slippers. She was my pupil and my teacher, my subject and my sovereign, my trusty comrade, friend, shipmate, fellow-soldier. My mistress, but at the same time all that any man friend has ever been to me.
>
> C. S. Lewis

Marriage is closer to the nature of God than any other human experience. God uses the metaphor of marriage to describe relating to humanity: "As a bridegroom rejoices over his bride, so will your God rejoice over you."[5] God loves the church, "the bride," says Paul, not as a group of people external to himself with whom he has entered into an agreement, but as his own body.[6] And similarly, when a husband loves his wife and a wife her husband, as extensions of themselves, they live as "one flesh"—as soul mates.

Finally, through marriage, God also shows himself in two important ways: first, by revealing his faithfulness, and second, by revealing his forgiveness.

MARRIAGE REVEALS GOD'S FAITHFULNESS

What would marriage be like without faithfulness? What if the best we could ever get from our partner was "I'll try to be true, but don't count on it." Of course, marriage would never survive. We would go insane with uncertainty if we could not count on our mate's faithfulness. The livelihood of our relationship depends on the strength of faithfulness—theirs, ours, and ultimately God's.

Yes, God's faithfulness is essential to the survival of our marriages. Think about it. How can we, weak and limited persons that we are, look all the uncertainty of life full in the face and say, "I will make one thing certain: my faithfulness to my partner"? We can't, at least not on our own.

> Marriage is a partnership in which each inspires the other.
>
> Millicent Carey McIntosh

Robertson McQuilkin is a husband who is known for relying on God's faithfulness. He was a Christian college president and his wife, Muriel, was the host of a successful radio program when Muriel began to experience memory failure. The medical diagnosis turned their forty-two-year marriage inside out. Muriel had Alzheimer's.

"It did not seem painful to her," said Robertson, "but it was a slow dying for me to watch the creative, articulate person I knew and loved gradually dimming out." Robertson approached his college board of trustees and asked them to begin the search for his successor, telling them that when the day came that Muriel needed him full-time, she would have him.

Because Robertson still had eight years to go before retirement, his friends urged him to arrange for the institutionalization of Muriel. She will become accustomed to her new environment quickly, they said. *But would she?* Robertson asked himself. *Would anyone love her at all, let alone love her as I do?* Muriel could not speak in sentences, only words, and often words that made little sense. But she could say one sentence, and she said it often: "I love you."

The college board arranged for a companion to stay with Muriel so Dr. McQuilkin could go daily to his office. During that time it became increasingly difficult to keep Muriel home. When Robertson left, she would take out after him. The walk to the college was a mile round-trip from their house, and Muriel would make the trip as many as ten times a day. "Sometimes at night," said Robertson, "when I helped her undress, I found bloody feet. When I told our family doctor, he choked up and simply said, 'Such love.'"

In 1990, believing that being faithful to Muriel "in sickness and in health" was a matter of integrity, Robertson McQuilkin resigned his presidency to care for his wife full-time. "Daily, I discern new manifestations of the kind of person she is," he has said. "I also see fresh manifestations of God's love—the God I long to love more fully."

Several years have passed since Robertson's resignation, and Muriel has steadily declined so that now she rarely speaks. She sits most of the time, while he writes, yet she is contented and often bubbles with laughter. "She seems still to have affection for me," says Robertson. "What more could I ask? I have a home full of love and laughter; many couples with their wits about them don't have that! Muriel is very lovable—more dear to me now than ever. When she reaches out to me in the night hours or smiles contentedly and lovingly as she awakes, I thank the Lord for his grace to us and ask him to let me keep her."

Faithfulness is like a multifaceted jewel, exhibiting a complex combination of interrelated dimensions—trust, commitment, truth, loyalty, valuing, care. But our faithfulness to each other can only be sustained by God's model of faithfulness to us. When a man and woman covenant with one another, God promises faithfulness to them. And that helps couples keep the faith.

There is no way to overemphasize the centrality of faithfulness in God's character. It is woven into every part of the Bible—from Genesis, where God initiates his promise of faithfulness, through Revelation, where John's vision depicts "a white horse whose rider is called Faithful and True." Great is God's faithfulness. Even when we are faithless, God will remain faithful, "for he cannot disown himself."[7]

God's covenantal faithfulness, embodied in our partner, makes a home for our restless hearts. It accepts our whole soul by saying, "I believe in you and commit myself to you through thick and thin." Without faithfulness and the trust it engenders, marriage would have no hope of enduring. For no couple can achieve deep confidence in the fidelity of themselves and each other until they first recognize God's faithfulness to them.

MARRIAGE REVEALS GOD'S FORGIVENESS

While we were living in Los Angeles, a friend invited us to tour the Hollywood film studio where she worked. We rode across the lot on a handy golf cart and quietly ducked into sound stages to catch behind-the-scene glimpses of familiar faces. One of the highlights was watching the filming of an episode of the hit TV show "thirtysomething." Our friend, observing our interest in this particular show, later sent us an autographed script. It featured Nancy and Elliot, a struggling married couple, in a brutal counseling session. Finally Elliot says, "I don't know if I love Nancy anymore.... And no matter what she does, I can't seem to forgive her for that."

Forgiveness lies at the heart of marriage. Two people living together, day after day, stumbling over each other's beings, are bound to cause pain, sometimes innocently, sometimes not. And if forgiveness is not given to cleanse the marriage soul, condemnation hovers over the relationship. Resentment piles on top of resentment until we blame our partners not just for their wrongdoing, but for our failure to forgive them, too.

This is a red-light danger zone. Human forgiveness was never designed to be given on a grand scale. Forgiveness in marriage can only heal when the focus is on what our spouses *do*, not on who they *are*. Partners forgive best for specific acts. Trying to forgive carte blanche is silly. Nobody can do that but God.

We overload the circuits of forgiveness when we try to forgive our partner for not being the sort of partner we want him or her to be. There are other means for coping with this disappointment: courage, empathy, patience, hope. But for mere human beings, forgiveness in the grand manner must be left to God. For it is God's forgiveness that empowers our ability to forgive the relatively small things—no minor miracle in itself.

> To keep your marriage brimming, With love in the loving cup, Whenever you're wrong, admit it; Whenever you're right, shut up.
>
> Ogden Nash

Every couple needs to forgive. I (Leslie) had a hard time accepting that. Why would I ever need to forgive Les, the man who had pledged his love to me unto death? Somehow I thought that if forgiveness was necessary, our relationship was failing. I was too proud to admit that Les could hurt me. But at times he did. And of course, I hurt him. In fact, I have learned that most of the time, forgiveness in marriage is usually not about an innocent lamb and a bad wolf. Most of the time I have to do my forgiving while being forgiven—by God, if not by my husband.

When we forgive a partner, we are revealing God's love to him or her, free from condemnation. Human forgiveness enlightens divine forgiveness.

Loving your partner as yourself is probably the single most wholehearted step you will ever take to fulfill the love of God. Such a step, of course, could never even be contemplated without the enabling grace of God. While many marriages are undertaken,

> Anyone without a soul friend is like a body without a head.
>
> Celtic saying

and even manage to last, without a conscious reliance on God's help, there are no meaningful partnerships without the continuing secret touch of God's grace on the soul of their marriage.

TENDING THE SOUL OF YOUR MARRIAGE

Superficiality is the curse of a restless marriage. The desperate need of most marriages is not for more excitement, more glitz, more activity. The soul of your marriage yearns for depth.

At least three classic disciplines of the spiritual life call soul mates to move beyond surface living and into the depths: worship, service, and prayer. In the midst of our normal daily activities, these disciplines have a transforming power to quiet the spirit and nurture our marriage.[8] By the way, these disciplines are not for spiritual giants, nor are they some dull drudgery designed to extinguish all the fun in your life. The only requirement to practice these disciplines is a longing for God to fill your marriage.

WORSHIP

We have a Norman Rockwell print that depicts a family on Sunday morning. The husband, unshaven, messy-haired, and ensconced in pajamas and bathrobe, is slumped in a chair with portions of the Sunday paper strewn about. Behind him is his wife, dressed in a tailored suit and on her way to church. The picture is a playful reminder to us of how important shared worship is to the soul of our marriage.

Both of us grew up going to church. It was a part of our heritage. As surely as the sun came up in the east, our families would be in church on Sunday morning. Going to church wasn't questioned. It was just something you did. Case closed.

But when we got married and moved far from home, worship was suddenly an option. In a new city, we were faced with the opportunity of establishing our own routines, our own weekly patterns. For the first time, going to church was something we were not compelled to do. Nobody was going to call and ask where we were. Nobody was checking up on us. We could now stay home on Sundays, take a hike, sit in the sun, read a book. Or we could go to church. We did.

From the beginning of our marriage, shared worship has been a systematic time of rest and renewal for our relationship. Dedicating a day of the week to worship stabilizes our marriage and liberates us from the tyranny of productivity that fills our other days.

The church where we worship is a place of social support and spiritual refueling. Singing hymns, learning from Scripture, worshiping God, and meeting with friends who share our spiritual quest is comforting and inspiring. Worshiping together buoys our relationship and makes the week ahead more meaningful.

> As the deer pants for streams of water, so my soul pants for you, O God. My soul thirsts for God.
>
> Psalm 42:1 – 2

And once again, research supports our decision to worship together as a means of nurturing the soul of our marriage. A recent study showed that couples who attended church together even as little as once a month increase their chances of staying married for life. Studies have also shown that churchgoers feel better about their marriages than those who don't worship together.[9]

Worship has a way of transforming relationships. To stand before the Holy One of eternity is to grow and change. In worship, God's transforming power steals its way into the sanctuary of our hearts and enlarges our capacity to love.

SERVICE

"I never knew how selfish I was until I got married," said Gary. After six months of marriage, he was telling us how Paula, his wife, was volunteering at a retirement center one night a week. "At first I resented her being away from me. But a couple of months ago she needed a lift, so I went with her." He came back with Paula again and again, until he discovered that helping the older people at the center had become the highlight of his week. "It feels good to help others, and it brings Paula and me closer together; it's like we are a team that is making a difference," he told us.

> Love does not consist in gazing at each other but in looking together in the same direction.
>
> Antoine de Saint-Exupéry

We have heard dozens of similar reports from couples. There is something good about reaching out as a team. Almost mystically it becomes bonding. Reaching out to others promotes humility, sharing, compassion, and intimacy in a marriage. Doing good for others helps couples transcend themselves and become part of something larger.[10]

There are literally hundreds of ways to incorporate shared service into your marriage. The key is to find something that fits your personal style. For example, we have two couples in our neighborhood who both actively practice reaching out, but in different ways. Steve and Thanne Moore live in the house across the street from us and have been married fifteen years. They sponsor a needy child, Robert Jacques, who lives in Haiti. Every month they send him cards and letters as well as money to provide education, clothes, and food. On special occasions, Steve and Thanne will have their three children draw pictures to send to Robert. Twice, Steve and Thanne have even traveled to Haiti to be with Robert at his orphanage. Someday, they hope to see him in college.

Two blocks down the street in our neighborhood live Dennis and

Lucy Guernsey. They have been married twenty-five years, and from the beginning they made a joint decision: to have an open home and be generous with others. Everyone who knows Dennis and Lucy knows of their hospitality. They have made their home a hub of celebration and delicious dinners. Sometimes it's casual and spontaneous, sometimes planned and elegant, but always, it is special. They throw graduation parties, birthday parties, welcome-to-the-neighborhood parties. They hold showers and receptions. And on Mother's Day they invite single moms for Sunday brunch.

If you ask either Dennis and Lucy or Steve and Thanne why they reach out the way they do, they will tell you how fulfilling it is to make others happy. But they will also tell you about the deep bond their shared service brings to their own marriage.

We know lots of couples who can testify to how meaningful reaching out to others is to their marriage. Whether it be sponsoring a needy child, opening your home to guests, giving blankets to the homeless, or baking cookies for prisoners, doing good for others is good for your marriage. For soul mates, true service is not self-righteous, it's not done for rewards, it's not a "big deal." It comes from whispered promptings, divine urgings deep within the soul of your marriage.

> Love is like a tennis match; you'll never win consistently until you learn to serve well.
>
> Dan P. Herod

One more thing about serving together. If all of your service is before others, it will remain shallow. Service is sometimes done in secret, concealed from everyone but the two of you. We find that the soul of our marriage is satisfied most when we do something, even small things, anonymously. To secretly observe the results of our service brings deeper devotion and intimacy.

Workbook Exercise 27
Improving Your Serve

Reaching out to others can do more to strengthen a marriage bond than you might ever imagine. The workbook exercise *Improving Your Serve* will help you and your partner explore how you might incorporate service into your partnership.

Tending the soul of your marriage requires constant attention. For if you neglect the soul of your marriage there will be only superficial bonding, which rides the waves of emotion and infatuation until the marriage is beached. But if in your sojourn together you tend the soul—through worship, service, and prayer—you will make it through the storms of marriage unscathed.

PRAYER

Sociologist Andrew Greeley surveyed married people and found that the happiest couples were those who pray together. Couples who frequently pray together are twice as likely as those who pray less often to describe their marriages as being highly romantic. They also report considerably higher sexual satisfaction and more sexual ecstasy!

There is an old story about a young couple who decided to start their honeymoon by kneeling beside their bed to pray. The bride giggled when she heard her new husband's prayer. "For what we are about to receive may the Lord make us truly thankful."

As strange as it may sound, there is a strong link in marriage between prayer and sex. For one thing, frequency of prayer is a more powerful predictor of marital satisfaction than frequency of sexual intimacy. But get this: Married couples who pray together are 90 percent more likely to report higher satisfaction with their sex life than couples who do not pray together. Also, women who pray with their partner tend to be more orgasmic. That doesn't sound right, does it? After all, married churchgoers are painted by the media as prudes who think sex is dirty. Well, let the media say what they want, but prayerful couples know better.

Few couples have come into our office who are more devout than Tom and Kathleen. They attended church regularly. Kathleen sang in the choir; Tom taught junior high Sunday school. Kathleen was in a women's Bible study; Tom was in a men's accountability group. Everyone in their church looked to Tom and Kathleen as dedicated and vibrant spiritual leaders. But when the two of them came to see us, their five-year-old marriage was falling apart at the seams. They told us their story, one we had heard many times. They were overinvolved with everything but their marriage and as a result had "fallen out of love." In spite of all their spiritual fervor, Tom and Kathleen had allowed the soul of their marriage to wither.

"When was the last time the two of you prayed together?" one of us asked. Tom and Kathleen looked at each other, and the answer was obvious: It had been a long, long time.

We talked with Tom and Kathleen a bit longer and gave them a simple assignment, an experiment really. For the next week they were to pray briefly together just before going to bed.

Five days later we received a call. "This is Kathleen. I know this sounds crazy, but our relationship has done an about-face." She told us how spending a moment together in prayer was rejuvenating their spirits and their marriage.

No amount of being "religious" can make up for the time couples spend in shared prayer. But if prayer is so good for a marriage, you may be asking, why don't more couples do it? Because it's not easy. Praying is vulnerable, and anytime we let our guard down, even with our spouse, it can be threatening (this is especially true for men). After all, our partner knows, firsthand, what we are really like. He or she sees us when nobody else is watching. So how can

I be completely candid before God with my partner listening in?

How can I express my true hopes and fears, my pain, the sins that grip me? No wonder many couples opt out of prayer. The price of its vulnerability seems too high.

Praying together as a couple, we must confess, has not always been natural or easy for Leslie and me. We have at times both fallen into the trap of preaching through our prayers and subtly jabbing each other with our "good" intentions. But through the years we have picked up some principles that have helped us pray more effectively. First, we pray a prayer of thanksgiving. That's all. Rather than trying to pray about our needs or difficulties, we simply give thanks to God. Occasionally we say the Lord's Prayer together (Matthew 6:9–13). And sometimes one of us will simply initiate a time of silent prayer together or a time of listening to God or maybe a time of brief sentence prayers. The point is to pray. There is no right or wrong way to do it. Every attempt we make to commune with God in shared prayer nurtures the soul of our marriage.

Workbook Exercise 28
Study Your Spouse

While praying with each other is important in a marriage, praying for each other is also crucial. The workbook exercise *Study Your Spouse* will help you pray more meaningfully for your spouse.

SO REMEMBER THIS

Like most couples deeply in love, we longed to be soul mates even before we were married. Part of the impetus for our vision came from reading *A Severe Mercy*, the real-life love story about Sheldon and Davy Vanauken, two lovers who not only dreamed about building a soulful union but devised a concrete strategy for doing so called their

Shining Barrier. Its goal: to make their love invulnerable. Its plan: to share *everything*. Everything! If one of them liked something, they decided, there must be something to like in it—and the other must find it. Whether it be poetry, strawberries, or an interest in ships, Sheldon and Davy committed to share every single thing either of them liked. That way they would create a thousand strands, great and small, that would link them together. They reasoned that by sharing everything they would become so close that it would be impossible, unthinkable, for either of them to suppose that they could ever recreate such closeness with anyone else. Total sharing, they felt, was the ultimate secret of a love that would last forever.

To be the watch upon the walls of the Shining Barrier, Sheldon and Davy established what they called the Navigators' Council. It was an inquiry into the state of their union. Were they fully sharing? Was there any sign of growing apart? More than once a month they would intentionally talk about their relationship and evaluate their activities by asking: Is this best for our love?

Something about this Shining Barrier—a shield to protect one's love and build a fortified bond—appealed to Leslie and me. We wanted to guard against losing the glory of love. We did not fear divorce as much as we feared a more subtle enemy—gradual separateness. Looking about us, we saw marriages perishing because the couples took love for granted. Ceasing to do things together, finding separate interests, couples we knew were turning "we" into "I" as their marriages aged. We observed a subtle separateness creeping into their marriage with barely a notice—each of them going off to their separate jobs in separate worlds, while their apartness was quietly tearing at their union. Why let this happen to us? Why not raise the Shining Barrier as Sheldon and Davy did?

We were inspired.

Late in the spring, just days before our wedding, we sat on a bench talking about our love and impending commitment and concluded that there was something cold about making a contractual agreement, a binding commitment, to stay together. We didn't want to perform marital "duties" because we *had* to, because we were locked into it externally. We were looking for a deeper bond that transcended even the idealized vestiges of the Shining Barrier. That's when the real lesson of Sheldon and Davy's story hit us: that becoming soul mates ultimately requires more than an appeal to love, more than a commitment to extravagant sharing. It requires an appeal to God.

The aching, burning urge you and your partner have to be connected—soul to soul—can only be quenched when your spirits are joined by a greater Spirit, Jesus Christ—the ultimate Shining Barrier. So remember this: The sacred secret to becoming soul mates is pursuing a mutual communion with God.

FOR REFLECTION

1. Some couples confuse being "exactly" alike or having a "fifty-fifty" marriage with being soul mates. Why is this not really accurate?

2. There is an aching in our souls that longs for deeper meaning and connection with our partner and with God. In what ways do you see people trying to quench this thirst of their spirit? What are the positive and negative ways people try to meet this need?

3. In what ways have you seen God revealed in your relationship?

4. Praying together can be difficult for couples. Sometimes one partner feels more comfortable with it or more eager to do it than the other, and this imbalance can make the other partner "prayer shy." How do you see this spiritual discipline being a part of your marriage?

5. How can couples tend the soul of their marriages through shared service? Do you know of couples who practice this discipline? In what ways could you incorporate service into your marriage?

Appendix

DISCOVERING YOUR PERSONALITY DYNAMICS

---

*The meeting of two personalities is like the
contact of two chemical substances; if there
is any reaction, both are transformed.*

CARL GUSTAV JUNG

Every marriage relationship is unprecedented. Every couple is unique. There has never been a marriage like the one you're starting. When two personalities come together, the combination of your dynamics creates a unique blend of characteristics and qualities. The better you understand your combination of traits, the more likely you are to appreciate them and use them to your advantage.

It's what caused German poet Heinrich Heine to liken marriage to "the high sea for which no compass has yet been invented!" Sure there are universal techniques and strategies that can help nearly every couple—empathy is a good example. What married relationship couldn't benefit from more of that? But implementing a technique or strategy for more empathy becomes a challenge that hinges on that couple's combined personalities.

WHY YOU NEED TO KNOW YOUR PERSONALITY DYNAMIC

Every autumn semester for many years running, I (Les) have taught a university class called Personality. You'll find this course in every undergraduate curriculum for psychology majors in every college in the country. Scholars agree that this information is essential to a basic education in the science of psychology.

We have come to believe that this information should also be required study for anyone who gets married. Why? Because understanding your personality dynamics can often make the difference between sinking and swimming in marriage.

> We come to love not by finding a perfect person but by learning to see an imperfect person perfectly.
>
> Sam Keen

The word "personality" originates from the Latin *persona*, which means "mask." And all of us can't help but to wear a mask of sorts when we first enter into a dating relationship.

Think about the first date the two of you had. Maybe you went to a nice dinner. We had ours at the Magic Pan in Kansas City on the famed Plaza. Perhaps you went to a movie or a concert, played mini golf, or attended a ball game. You can probably recall what you were wearing. Maybe even what you had for dinner. You may even recollect what you talked about. And you may be able to conjure up some of the feelings you had on that first date.

Why? Because, if you are like most people, you put a lot of energy into it. You worked hard to create a positive impression of who you were for this person whom you eventually decided to marry. Even if you decided at the outset that you were just going to be yourself, you couldn't help feeling a bit of pressure to "perform" and to be the best *you* possible.

It's commonly believed that nearly everyone wears some sort of a mask on their first few dates. They may wear a mask for some time, wanting to continue a charade of the very best version of themselves. Some would argue that mask wearing may even continue into the first bit of marriage.

But sooner or later, the masks for both people come off. The real person is revealed. We see what they do when they are hurt, angry, jealous, annoyed, and so on. It can't be helped. If you are with someone long enough in varying circumstances, you gradually discover the actual person. That's why some say, love is blind, but marriage restores its sight.

HOW DO YOUR PERSONALITIES MESH?

We have a friend, Jim Gwinn, who often tells engaged couples he's counseling, "Just remember: What is now, will be then, only more so." It's his way of saying that whatever you find a bit annoying about your fiancée during your engagement will not disappear after you marry. Quite the opposite! It's safe to say that he or she is actually tempering that quality and you won't see its full manifestation until months from now when you are husband and wife.

That's why a close examination of a couple's combined personality dynamics is essential for effective marriage preparation. Your personalities influence everything in your marriage. They influence your thinking, attitudes, motivations, expectations, and behaviors. In short, they influence how you give and receive love.

It's difficult to exaggerate how much your two unique personalities will shape your experience of married life together.

Unfortunately, it is impossible to do this topic justice through the pages of a book. Your two personalities are far too complicated. That's one of the primary reasons we designed the SYMBIS Assessment. More than half of the personalized, fifteen-page report is dedicated to helping you see everything from communication and conflict to sex and money through the lens of your two unique personalities—and how they can be leveraged for maximizing your love for each other.

It begins by helping you uncover what kind of spouse each of you tends to be:

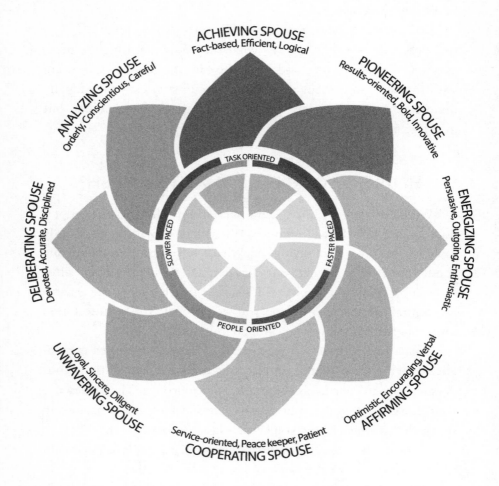

As you can see, you can land in one of eight different personality types. And even when you land in one of them, your personality is far too unique to be summarized by a label or even a paragraph. That's why the SYMBIS Assessment provides you with several pages of information about your two personalities—and even if you're the same overall personality type, you'll have differences within them.[1]

Here's a quick and cursory snapshot of each:

- *Achieving Spouse:* Fact-based, efficient, and logical
- *Pioneering Spouse:* Results-oriented, bold, and innovative
- *Energizing Spouse:* Persuasive, outgoing, and enthusiastic
- *Affirming Spouse:* Optimistic, encouraging, and verbal
- *Cooperating Spouse:* Service-oriented, peace keeper, and patient
- *Unwavering Spouse:* Loyal, sincere, and diligent
- *Deliberating Spouse:* Devoted, accurate, and disciplined
- *Analyzing Spouse:* Orderly, conscientious, and careful

One personality type is not any better or worse than any other. They are simply different. And that's where far too many couples get bogged down. They don't appreciate, let alone understand, their personality differences.

Not only that, they don't understand how they play off of each other. It is one thing to discover how each of your two personalities are depicted, but your love goes to a whole new level once you both see what happens when your two personalities mesh. For example, what happens when an Affirming Spouse marries an Analyzing Spouse? This kind of information about your two personalities is exactly what's unpacked in the SYMBIS Assessment.

> There is little difference in people, but that little difference makes a big difference.
>
> W. Clement Stone

YOUR PERSONALITIES ARE GOD-GIVEN

You can't choose your personality like you choose your wardrobe. Relatively speaking, you have just one personality for life. It is something you are born with. Sure, you can modify portions of your personality, and your response to your environment can cultivate or stifle aspects of it. But by and large, your personality represents your natural traits or tendencies.

Ask any mother who has raised at least two children, and chances are she will tell you that they were different from the beginning. For example, one child may have been very friendly and smiled at everyone; whereas, the other was always frightened when strangers were present. They were each born that way.

> The goal in marriage is not to think alike but to think together.
>
> Robert C. Dodds

The point is that your personality is in your genes. It is inborn. It is God-given. You inherited a distinctive set of traits that are fundamental to your nature.

Surely you've heard your spouse say something like, "That's just not you." You might think this when your boss has asked you to greet everyone as they enter a social gathering—and your personality just isn't cut out for that. Do you do what your boss asks? You do if you want to keep your job. But it feels awkward. The point is that you *can* behave in a way that does not represent your personality, but this will always be temporary. Any number of situations may require that you behave in a way that is not natural for you to act, but when the need has passed, you will once again act in a way that represents your true temperament. That's because your personality is innate.

GETTING THE LOVE YOU WANT

Violet Bailey and her fiancé Samuel Booth were strolling through the English countryside in 1941, deeply in love and engaged to be married. A diamond engagement ring sparkled on Violet's finger—her most treasured possession.

But, as can happen with couples, something was said that hurt the other's feelings and an argument ensued, then escalated. At its worst point, Violet became so angry she pulled the diamond engagement ring from her finger, drew back her arm, and hurled the treasured possession with all her might into the field. The ring sailed through the air, fell to the ground, and nestled under the grass in such a way that it was impossible to see.

Violet and Samuel eventually made up. Their argument, both agreed, was foolish. Desperate to recover their lost ring, they walked and walked through that field hunting for it. But they never found it.

Two months later, they were married. They had a child and eventually a grandson. Part of their family lore was the story of the lost engagement ring. Everyone knew about it even decades later.

Violet and Samuel grew old together, and in 1993 Samuel died. Fifteen years passed, but the ring was not forgotten. One day Violet's grandson got an idea. Perhaps he could find his grandmother's ring with a metal detector. With a newly purchased detector in hand, he went to the field where Violet had hurled her treasured possession sixty-seven years earlier. He turned on the machine and began to crisscross the field, waving the detector over the grass. After two hours of searching, he finally found what he was looking for.

Later, with immense joy and pride, the grandson placed the diamond ring into the hand of his astonished grandmother Violet. The treasured possession had finally come home.[2]

> Mutual empathy is the great unsung human gift.
>
> Jean Baker Miller

Can you imagine finally discovering what you've been hoping to find for more than six decades? The story, of course, is bittersweet. While the ring was found, Samuel didn't get to finally place that lost ring on her finger. Violet got was she was looking for, but most would say it was much too late.

Don't let the same thing happen in your marriage. We're not talking about losing a ring, of course. We're talking about something far more priceless. We're talking about losing days that turn into years where you don't get the love you want.

We've written this Appendix and created the online SYMBIS Assessment to ensure that this doesn't happen to you. By taking a deep look at your inner hardwiring for love, you will enter each other's worlds. You'll know how you can be a better spouse with your particular hardwiring and how you can better love your spouse with theirs.

In short, knowing how your personalities mesh gives you a sophisticated tool for empathy—that capacity to see the world from each other's perspective. And why does this matter? Because empathy is at the heart of every healthy marriage. It's what allows you to walk in each other's shoes without stepping on each other's toes.

Hundreds of research studies have pointed to the immeasurable value of empathy in marriage. And with a deep understanding of your combined personalities, you'll have one of the greatest means for enjoying it in yours.

> Love is the condition in which the happiness of another person is essential to your own.
>
> Robert Heinlein

ACKNOWLEDGMENTS

WE ARE DEEPLY INDEBTED to many individuals who contributed to the *Saving Your Second Marriage Before It Starts* project. The people at Zondervan, as always, were extraordinary. We have been blessed by more than one visionary publisher on this project: Scott Bolinder and David Morris. Our long-time editor, Sandy Vander Zicht, and her associates, Lori Walburg Vanden Bosch, Becky Shingledecker Philpott, and Greg Clouse, are not only professionally gifted but personally invested. We are also grateful to so many others on our publishing team: Tom Dean, Robin Barnett, Catherine DeVries, Larry Downs, Casper Hamlet, Joyce Ondersma, John Topliff, TJ Rathbun, and John Raymond. Special thanks to our dear friends at Flying Rhino: Chris and Toni Crary and the incredible Ranjy Thomas. And our team that keeps everything humming: Janice Lundquist, David Huffman, Sealy Yates, Mandi Moragne, and Ryan Farmer.

In the process of writing this book, we have become acutely aware of the intellectual giants on whose shoulders we stand. Scholars like John Gottman at the University of Washington, Howard Markman and Scott Stanley at the University of Denver, Clifford Notarious at The Catholic University of America in Washington, D.C., Deborah Tannen at Georgetown University, David Olson at the University of Minnesota, Robert and Jeanette Lauer at U.S. International University in San Diego, Robert Sternberg at Yale University, and Everett Worthington at Virginia Commonwealth University, just to name a few. To all of them, we are deeply grateful.

Finally, we want to express our appreciation to the thousands of SYMBIS Facilitators who help couples successfully launch lifelong love, as well as the couples who have participated in our *Saving Your Marriage Before It Starts* seminars. To be a part of your journey has been an honor.

NOTES

BEFORE YOU BEGIN

1. These findings are based on a nationwide study of 455 newlyweds and 75 longer-married people looking back on their first year of marriage. The research is published in Miriam Arond and Samuel L. Pauker's book, *The First Year of Marriage* (New York: Warner, 1987).

2. These findings are based on telephone interviews with 1,037 adults, age eighteen and above. The survey was conducted between September 24 and October 9, 1988. Error attributable to sampling and other random effects could be plus or minus four percentage points.

3. The technical measure for divorce rates is called "age-standardized refined divorce rate" (psychobabble, for sure). It's what's used for aggregate measures by the U.S. Census Bureau. The best summary of the often complicated depiction of divorce rates that we know of was written by Dr. Scott Stanley for the Institute for Family Studies on January 22, 2015. See http://slidingvsdeciding .blogspot.com/search?q=divorce+rate.

4. Galatians 5:22–23 MSG.

QUESTION ONE: ARE YOU READY TO GET MARRIED AGAIN?

1. E. H. Walster, "The Effects of Self-Esteem on Romantic Linking," *Journal of Experimental and Social Psychology* 1 (1965): 184–97.

2. S. J. Katz and A. E. Liu, *False Love and Other Romantic Illusions: Why Love Goes Wrong and How to Make It Right* (New York: Ticknor and Fields, 1988).

3. B. Lott, *Women's Lives: Themes and Variations in Gender Learning* (Monterey, Calif.: Brooks/Cole, 1987).

4. J. F. Crosby, *Illusion and Disillusion: The Self in Love and Marriage*, 4th ed. (Belmont, Calif.: Wadsworth, 1991).

5. D. H. Knox Jr., *Marriage: Who? When? Why?* (Englewood Cliffs, N.J.: Prentice-Hall, 1975).

6. K. Grover, "Mate Selection Processes and Marital Satisfaction," *Family Relations* 34 (1985): 383–86. Quoted in Neil Clark Warren's *Finding the Love of Your Life* (Colorado Springs: Focus on the Family, 1992).

7. S. White and C. Hatcher, "Couple Complementarity and Similarity: A Review of the Literature," *The American Journal of Family Therapy* 12 (1984): 15–25.

8. Note: Among couples having age differences of ten years or fewer, there are very few significant differences in marital quality. However, in marriages in which the husband is eleven or more years older than his wife, marital problems concerning money, friends, and so on, are more likely. H. Vera, D. Berardo, and F. Berardo, "Age Heterogamy in Marriage," *Journal of Marriage and the Family* 47 (1985): 553–66.

9. J. Daw, "Love's Illusions," *Monitor on Psychology* (March 2001): 15.

QUESTION TWO: HAVE YOU FACED THE MYTHS OF REMARRIAGE WITH HONESTY?

1. J. H. Larson, "The Marriage Quiz: College Students' Beliefs in Selected Myths about Marriage," *Family Relations* 37, no. 1 (1988): 43–51. A study of couples married an average of one year found that almost every couple suffered severe disappointment within a few months after marriage because of their misconceptions about marriage. These results echo the findings of W. Lederer and D. Jackson in *The Mirages of Marriage* (New York: Norton, 1968).

2. Mike Mason, *The Mystery of Marriage* (Portland, Oreg.: Multnomah, 1985), 31.

3. M. Scott Peck, *The Road Less Traveled: A New Psychology of Love, Traditional Values, and Spiritual Growth* (New York: Simon & Schuster, 1978), 84–85. Dr. Peck also writes: "Of all the misconceptions about love the most powerful and pervasive is the belief that 'falling in love' is love.... It is a potent misconception. The experience of falling in love is specifically a sex-linked erotic experience.... We fall in love only when we are consciously or unconsciously sexually motivated."

4. All lovers engage in a game of make-believe where they try to appear more emotionally healthy than they really are. As Harville Hendrix has said, "After all, if you don't appear to have many needs of your own, your partner is free to assume that your goal in life is to nurture, not to be nurtured, and this makes you very desirable indeed." *Getting the Love You Want* (New York: HarperCollins, 1990), 45.

5. John Levy and R. Munroe, *The Happy Family* (New York: Knopf, 1959).

6. J. F. Crosby, *Illusion and Disillusion: The Self in Love and Marriage*, 2nd ed. (Belmont, Calif.: Wadsworth, 1976). Also O. Kernberg, "Why Some People Can't Love," *Psychology Today* (February, 1988): 44–47).

7. H. E. Marano, "Divorced? Don't Even Think of Remarrying Until You Read This," *Psychology Today* 33, no. 2 (March/April 2000): 57–62.

8. Proverbs 27:17.

9. J. F. Crosby, *Illusion and Disillusion: The Self in Love and Marriage*.

10. Deuteronomy 24:5.

CHAPTER THREE: CAN YOU IDENTIFY YOUR LOVE STYLE?

1. This is not a new phenomenon. A poll taken in 1966 reported that 76 percent of the married couples questioned named "love" as the major reason for marrying. Ten years later, in 1976, when a psychologist asked 75,000 wives to evaluate the reasons for their decision to wed, she reported: "Love, love, love was far and away the front-runner." Paul Chance, "The Trouble with Love," *Psychology Today* (February 1988): 44–47.

2. L. Wrightsman and K. Deaux, *Social Psychology in the Eighties* (Monterey, Calif.: Brooks/Cole, 1981), 170.

   In the thirty-four years between 1949 and 1983, only twenty-seven articles on love appeared in professional journals of sociology and psychology, and each one was a professional risk for its author. When sociologist Nelson Foote, for example, published a short paper in 1953 entitled "Love," he was ridiculed and inundated with letters from other scholars, who declared him too sentimental.

   A panelist at the Convention of the American Psychological Association declared: "The scientist, in even attempting to interject love into a laboratory situation, is by the very nature of the proposition dehumanizing the state we call love."

3. Robert Sternberg, "A Triangular Theory of Love," *Psychological Review* 93 (1986): 119–35.

4. Song of Songs 1:2.

5. Neil Clark Warren, *Finding the Love of Your Life* (Colorado Springs: Focus on the Family, 1992).

6. Paul Tournier, *The Meaning of Gifts* (Atlanta: John Knox Press, 1963).

7. Psychologist Marcia Lasswell and her colleagues analyzed thousands of responses to a questionnaire on love and identified the following love styles: best-friend love, game-playing love, logical love, romantic love, possessive love, and unselfish love. These styles, however, are not as applicable to love within the marriage partnership.

8. Anne Morrow Lindbergh, *Gift from the Sea* (New York: Pantheon, 1991), 100.

9. W. D. Manning, "Trends in Cohabitation: Twenty Years of Change, 1987–2010," National Center for Family and Marriage Research. Retrieved from http://www.bgsu.edu/content/dam/BGSU/college-of-arts-and-sciences/NCFMR/documents/FP/FP–13–12.pdf.

10. J. Vespa, J. M. Lewis, and R. M. Kreider, R. M. "America's Families and Living Arrangements," United States Census Bureau (2013).

11. http://nationalmarriageproject.org/reports/.

12. Scott M. Stanley, Paul R. Amato, Howard J. Markham, and Christine A. Johnson, "The Timing of Cohabitation and Engagement: Impact on First and Second Marriages," *Journal of Family Psychology*, 72(4): 906–918. 2010 August 1. doi:10.1111/j.1741–3737.2010.00738.x.

13. G. K. Rhoades and S. M. Stanley, "Before 'I Do': What Do Premarital Experiences Have to Do with Marital Quality among Today's Young Adults?" (Charlottesville, Va.: National Marriage Project, 2014).

14. Meg Jay, *The Defining Decade: Why Your Twenties Matter—And How to Make the Most of Them Now* (New York: Twelve, 2013).

15. B. J. Willoughby and J. S. Carroll, "Correlates of Attitudes toward Cohabitation: Looking at the Associations with Demographics, Relational Attitudes, and Dating Behavior," *Journal of Family Issues* 23(11), 1450–1476.

16. 1 Corinthians 6:16–17 MSG. Other passages that speak to the issue include: Genesis 2:18–25; John 4; 1 Corinthians 10:12–13; Ephesians 5:3; 1 Thessalonians 4:3–8; and Hebrews 13:4.

17. These stages are discussed in greater detail by several authors, including James Olthuis in *Keeping Our Troth* (San Francisco: Harper and Row, 1986), Susan Campbell in *The Couple's Journey: Intimacy as a Path to Wholeness* (San Luis Obispo, Calif.: Impact Publishers, 1980), and Liberty Kovacs in *Marital Development* (1991).

18. D. Knox, "Conceptions of Love at Three Developmental Levels," *The Family Coordinator* 19, no. 2 (1970): 151–57.

19. For more tips on cultivating romantic passion, see Norm Wright's book *Holding On to Romance* (Ventura, Calif.: Regal Books, 1992).

20. Research reported in John Cuber's *The Significant Americans* (New York: Appleton/Century, 1966) revealed similar findings.

21. Stacey Oliker, *Best Friends and Marriage* (Los Angeles: University of California Press, 1989).

22. Nick Stinnett, "Strengthening Families," paper presented at the National Symposium on Building Family Strengths, University of Nebraska, Lincoln, Nebraska.

23. Alfred Kinsey, Wardell Pomeroy, and Clyde Martin, *Sexual Behavior in the Human Male* (Philadelphia: W. B. Sanders, 1948), 544.

CHAPTER FOUR: HAVE YOU DEVELOPED THE HABIT OF HAPPINESS?

1. Mary Landis and Judson Landis, *Building a Successful Marriage* (Englewood Cliffs, N.J.: Prentice Hall, 1958).

Notes

2. L. Parrott and L. Parrott, *Making Happy: The Art and Science of a Happy Marriage* (Nashville: Worthy, 2014).

3. Allen Parducci, "Value Judgments: Toward a Relational Theory of Happiness," in *Attitudinal Judgment*, ed. J. Richard Eiser (New York: Springer-Verlag, 1984).

4. To understand the problem of Mary and Joseph, we have to know something about marriage customs in those days. A betrothal was the forerunner of the engagement in modern romances. At the betrothal, the couple was legally bound and could not be separated except by divorce. It could be a matter of years before they were married, and even the marriage ceremony itself covered several days or as long as a week. Relatives who came ninety miles on the back of a donkey wanted something more than a piece of sheet cake before they returned home! So they stayed around to catch up on family news, build their relationships with each other, and rejoice with the bride and groom. Only when the days of the marriage ritual were ended did the couple begin living together. For Mary, it was sometime after the betrothal and before the marriage that she became pregnant. This called for a major adjustment on both Mary's and Joseph's parts.

5. Resentment and blame sometimes combine to sabotage marital happiness. For example, when you displace the blame for past hurts onto your present partner, you are activating a dynamic that psychiatrist Ivan Boszormenyi-Nagy describes as "the revolving ledger." At certain periods in your life, someone or something hurts you, running up a series of emotional debts. Time passes. You walk through life's revolving door, and now you hand your spouse the bill. And you hold two hidden expectations. First: "Prove to me you are not the person who hurt me." In other words, "Make up to me for the past. Pay me back." And second: "If you do one thing that reminds me of that hurt, I will punish you." The emotional transfer is accomplished.

It is crucial to understand that this emotional transfer often does not take place early in a relationship. It sets in after a couple has known each other for some time—when you are disappointed and discover that what you expected or hoped for isn't happening.

6. David Myers, *The Pursuit of Happiness: Who Is Happy and Why* (New York: Morrow, 1992). And George Gallup Jr. and F. Newport, "Americans Widely Disagree on What Constitutes 'Rich'," *Gallup Poll Monthly* (July 1990): 28–36.

QUESTION FIVE: CAN YOU SAY WHAT YOU MEAN AND UNDERSTAND WHAT YOU HEAR?

1. H. J. Markman, "Prediction of Marital Distress: A Five-Year Follow-Up," *Journal of Consulting and Clinical Psychology* 49 (1981): 760–62.

2. Reported in a Gallup Poll conducted between September 24 and October 9, 1988.

3. J. K. Burgoon, "Mindfulness and Interpersonal Communication," *Journal of Social Issues* 12 (2000): 1–15.

4. Laurens Van der Post, *The Face Beside the Fire* (New York: William Morrow, 1953), 268.

5. Virginia Satir, *The New Peoplemaking*, rev. ed. (Mountain View, Calif.: Science and Behavior Books, 1988).

6. R. M. Sabatelli, R. Buck, and A. Dreyer, "Nonverbal Communication Accuracy in Married Couples: Relationship with Marital Complaints," *Journal of Personality and Social Psychology* 43, no. 5 (1982): 1088–97.

7. Paul Tournier, *To Understand Each Other* (Atlanta: John Knox Press, 1967), 29.

8. Deborah Tannen, *You Just Don't Understand: Men and Women in Conversation* (New York: Ballantine, 1990).

9. http://www.cnn.com/2013/01/10/health/kerner-social
   -relationship/.

10. http://www.scientificamerican.com/article/how-your-cell-phone
    -hurts-your-relationships/.

11. Helen Fisher, *Anatomy of Love* (New York: W. W. Norton, 1992).

QUESTION SIX: HAVE YOU BRIDGED THE GENDER GAP?

1. Benjamin Amponsah, "Gender Differences in Spatial Abilities and Spatial Ability among University Students in an Egalitarian Educational System," *Sex Roles* (1998).

2. Y. Aida and T. Falbo, "Relationships Between Marital Satisfaction, Resources, and Power Strategies," *Sex Roles* 24 (1991): 43–56.

3. Betty Friedan, *The Second State* (New York: Summit Books, 1986).

4. This simplistic distinction is actually derived from studying a vast assortment of biological, hormonal, anatomical, neurological, psychological, and social differences. See Julia Wood, *Gendered Lives: Communication, Gender, and Culture* (Belmont, Calif.: Wadsworth, 1994) and Susan Basow, *Gender: Stereotypes and Roles*, 3rd ed. (Pacific Grove, Calif.: Brooks/Cole, 1992).

5. There are a number of ways to state this fundamental difference. Walter Wangerin Jr., in *As for Me and My House*, says men tend to be "instrumental" while women tend to be "expressive." John Gray, in *Men Are from Mars, Women Are from Venus*, says men "contract," women "expand."

6. H. J. Markman and S. A. Kraft, "Men and Women in Marriage: Dealing with Gender Differences in Marital Therapy," *The Behavior Therapist* 12 (1989): 51–56.

7. Deborah Tannen, *You Just Don't Understand: Men and Women in Conversation* (New York: Ballantine, 1990).

8. A study of one hundred and thirty healthy, strong couples revealed that almost all of the husbands reported that their partner knew how to make them feel good about themselves. M. Lasswell and T. Lasswell, *Marriage and the Family* (Lexington, Mass.: Heath, 1982).

9. John Gray, *Men Are from Mars, Women Are from Venus* (New York: HarperCollins, 1992), 29.

QUESTION SEVEN: DO YOU KNOW HOW TO FIGHT A GOOD FIGHT?

1. H. J. Markman, "Constructive Marital Conflict Is Not an Oxymoron," *Behavioral Assessment* 13 (1991): 83–96.

2. H. J. Markman, S. Stanley, F. Floyd, K. Hahlweg, and S. Blumberg, "Prevention of Divorce and Marital Distress," *Psychotherapy Research* (1992).

3. E. Bader, "Do Marriage Preparation Programs Really Help?" (paper presented at the National Council on Family Relations Annual Conference, Milwaukee, Wisconsin, 1981).

4. E. L. Boroughs, "Love and Money," *U.S. News and World Report* (October 19, 1992): 54–60. G. Hudson, "Money Fights," *Parents* (February 1992): 75–79.

5. R. Reading, "Debt, Social Disadvantage and Maternal Depression," *Social Science and Medicine* 53 (2001): 441–54.

6. "What to Do Before You Say 'I Do,'" *PRNewswire*, October 10, 2005.

7. For more information about these four disastrous ways of interacting, see John Gottman's *Why Marriages Succeed or Fail* (New York: Simon and Schuster, 1994).

8. F. D. Cox, *Human Intimacy: Marriage, the Family, and Its Meaning* (New York: West, 1990).

9. C. Notarius and H. Markman, *We Can Work It Out: Making Sense of Marital Conflict* (New York: Putnam, 1993).

QUESTION EIGHT: DO YOU KNOW HOW TO BLEND A FAMILY?

1. As a general rule, the term *stepfamily* is preferred because it is consistent with the naming of all other family types. All other family types are defined by the parent-child relationships (e.g., biological, foster, adoptive, single-parent). While the choice of stepfamily is seen by some as negative, the Stepfamily Association of America hopes that through education, the term *stepfamily* will acquire a more positive, or at the very least a neutral, connotation. Referring to stepfamilies as "blended families" is troublesome to stepfamilies and the professionals who work with them because it does not describe either a family relationship or what happens when at least one partner to a marriage brings children from a prior relationship. Children actively balk at inferences that the stepfamily is to be considered their new family, eligible to demand their full attention and loyalty. They know they have divided loyalties. Parents must accept the reality that their children have lots of "parents" now, and the nurturing no longer comes from a traditional family structure. Instead of trying to blend everyone, it seems far better to help all individuals to understand the nature of the extended and expanded family, with various segments having permeable boundaries. It is not helpful for anyone in a stepfamily to pretend that they are blended. While the term *blended* is still used for convenience of communication, the concept itself precludes working together with the expanded family members.

2. Richard Stuart and Barbara Jacobson, *Second Marriage* (New York: W. W. Norton, 1985).

3. D. H. Christensen and K. D. Rettig, "The Relationship of Remarriage to Post-Divorce Co-Parenting," *Journal of Divorce and Remarriage* (1995): 24.

4. Family psychologist James Bray suggests that "monitoring" is an effective beginning role for stepparents. This involves observing the children's activities or interests, so as to support their efforts, show interest in them as people, and have something in common to talk about.

5. There is no legal relationship between stepparents and stepchildren and this lack of a legal relationship (they are not related by birth, adoptive, or foster parents) is another reason the role of a stepparent is difficult. There is a sense of having responsibility without authority. By the way, no legal relationship with a stepchild means that unless the stepparent has written authority, he or she can't authorize emergency medical care, have access to school records, or sign important documents. This requires written authority and can be secured by being granted a limited power of attorney by the biological parent.

6. The Stepfamily Association of America (stepfam.org, or call 1–800–735–0329) works to support stepfamilies and help them be successful by providing information, education, and advocacy for stepfamilies and those who work with them. This organization can point you to other helpful resources in this area. Also visit Ron L. Deal's website at www.smartstepfamilies.com for other stepparenting resources.

QUESTION NINE: ARE YOU AND YOUR PARTNER SOUL MATES?

1. E. F. Lauer, "The Holiness of Marriage: Some New Perspectives from a Recent Sacramental Theology," *The Journal of Ongoing Formation* 6 (1985): 215–26.

2. Anne Frank, *Anne Frank: The Diary of a Young Girl*, trans. B. M. Mooyaart (New York: Bantam, 1993), 150–151.

3. D. R. Leckey, "The Spirituality of Marriage: A Pilgrimage of Sorts," *The Journal of Ongoing Formation* 6 (1985): 227–40.

4. D. L. Fenell, "Characteristics of Long-Term First Marriages," *Journal of Mental Health Counseling* 15 (1993): 446–60.

5. Isaiah 62:5.

6. Not infrequently God is called "a jealous God" (Exodus 20:5; 34:14; Deuteronomy 4:25; 5:9; 6:15). This phrase may sound strange to modern ears, but there is a beautiful idea behind it. The picture is that of God as the passionate lover of our souls. Love is always exclusive; no one can be totally in love with two people at the same time. To say that God is a jealous God is to say that God is the lover of men and women, and that his heart can brook no rival, but that he must have the whole devotion of our hearts. The divine-human relationship is not that of king and subject, nor that of master and servant, nor that of owner and slave, nor that of judge and defendant, but that of lover and loved one, a relationship which can only be paralleled in the perfect marriage relationship between husband and wife.

7. 2 Timothy 2:13.

8. L. M. Foerster, "Spiritual Practices and Marital Adjustment in Lay Church Members and Graduate Theology Students," Dissertation, Graduate School of Psychology, Fuller Theological Seminary, Pasadena, California, 1984.

9. S. T. Ortega, "Religious Homogamy and Marital Happiness," *Journal of Family Issues* 2 (1988): 224–39.

10. D. A. Abbott, M. Berry, and W. H. Meredith, "Religious Belief and Practice: A Potential Asset in Helping Families," *Family Relations* (1990): 443–48.

APPENDIX: DISCOVERING YOUR PERSONALITY DYNAMICS

1. The SYMBIS Assessment actually involves an exploration of more than 19,860 different combinations of personality traits—so even if you share a "type" with your partner, the report depicts finer differences. No two personalities are ever the same.

2. "It Wasn't All Bad," *The Week* (2–15–08), 4.

GIVE THE VERY BEST TO

You won't find a more personalized and powerful pre-marriage assessment than SYMBIS.

"The SYMBIS Assessment rocks! We learned so much about our relationship and feel incredibly confident about our future together."
-Toni & Chris

Get your personalized 15-page report!

YOUR RELATIONSHIP

EVERYTHING YOU NEED TO KNOW ABOUT:

- **Your Personalities** – *discover your strengths*
- **Your Love Life** – *cultivate deeper passion*
- **Your Fight Types** – *discover your "hot topics"*
- **Your Talk Styles** – *crack your intimacy codes*
- **Your Money Methods** – *kick financial woes to the curb*

And so much more. **Plus***, it works seamlessly with the SYMBIS book and his/her workbooks.*

Take the assessment: **SYMBISassessment.com**

YOUR ONE-STOP SHOP FOR
PRE-MARRIAGE

We've got everything you need to launch lifelong love.

LesandLeslie.com

book

training

assessment

remarriage book

DVD

his & hers
workbooks

WORKBOOK FOR MEN
Includes 24 Self-Tests and Group Discussion Guide

SAVING YOUR
MARRIAGE
BEFORE IT STARTS
Seven Questions to Ask Before - and After - You Remarry

Drs. Les & Leslie Parrott
#1 *New York Times* Bestselling Authors

NEWLY EXPANDED EDITION

WORKBOOK FOR WOMEN
Includes 24 Self-Tests and Group Discussion Guide

SAVING YOUR
MARRIAGE
BEFORE IT STARTS
Seven Questions to Ask Before - and After - You Remarry

SYMBIS

Drs. Les & Leslie Parrott
#1 *New York Times* Bestselling Authors

NEWLY EXPANDED EDITION

SAVING YOUR
MARRIAGE
BEFORE IT STARTS

Seven Questions to Ask   SEVEN SESSIONS
Before - and After - You Marry

Drs. Les & Leslie Parrott

ZONDERVAN
DVD

Bible
studies

WORKBOOK FOR MEN
Includes 24 Self-Tests and Group Discussion Guide

SAVING YOUR
SECOND
MARRIAGE
BEFORE IT STARTS
Nine Questions to Ask Before - and After - You Remarry

SYMBIS

Drs. Les & Leslie Parrott
#1 *New York Times* Bestselling Authors

NEWLY EXPANDED EDITION

WORKBOOK FOR WOMEN
Includes 24 Self-Tests and Group Discussion Guide

SAVING YOUR
SECOND
MARRIAGE
BEFORE IT STARTS
Nine Questions to Ask Before - and After - You Remarry

SYMBIS

Drs. Les & Leslie Parrott
#1 *New York Times* Bestselling Authors

NEWLY EXPANDED EDITION

SAVING YOUR
SECOND
MARRIAGE
BEFORE IT STARTS

Nine Questions to Ask   NINE SESSIONS
Before - and After - You Marry

Drs. Les & Leslie Parrott

ZONDERVAN
DVD

remarriage
DVD

remarriage
workbooks